Internal Rhetorics

Internal Rhetorics

Toward a History and Theory of Self-Persuasion

Jean Nienkamp

Southern Illinois University Press
Carbondale and Edwardsville

Printed in the United States of America
04 03 02 01 4 3 2 1

Library of Congress Cataloging-in-Publication Data

Nienkamp, Jean.
Internal rhetorics : toward a history and theory of self-persuasion / Jean Nienkamp.
p. cm.
Includes bibliographical references and index.
1. Ethics. 2. Rhetoric—Philosophy. 3. Persuasion (Rhetoric) 4. Self-talk. I. Title.

BJ42 .N54 2001
128'.4—dc21 2001018401
ISBN 0-8093-2406-7 (alk. paper)

The paper used in this publication meets the minimum requirements of American National Standard for Information Sciences—Permanence of Paper for Printed Library Materials, ANSI Z39.48-1992. ∞

Dedicated to the memory of Wilma Robb Ebbitt (1918–2000), whose trenchant thinking and writing, warm mentorship, and fierce advocacy for the importance of teaching in the academy have inspired her Penn State progeny.

Contents

Preface

The Obvious

The biggest leap I take in this book is the title, *Internal Rhetorics,* by which I initiate a study of the persuasive techniques we use on ourselves. The term is intended to be obvious and paradoxical—and, by the end of the book, complex. Obvious, in that it relates to common locutions:

I'm trying to talk myself into . . .

I've been arguing with myself all day . . .

I just had to give myself a good talking-to . . .

It's only crazy to talk to yourself if you answer back.

Most people talk to themselves.[1] The quotations that preface each chapter illustrate the long-standing prevalence of this idea that people persuade themselves into moods or actions.[2]

What we tend to take for granted in common parlance has not made its way into rhetorical theory in a systematic way, however. All the writers I discuss in this book are canonical in one sense or another, and most imply, mention, or discuss the use of persuasion on oneself—but no one so far has connected the dots. The current rhetorical community has hardly addressed self-persuasion, even though talking to oneself is at least as ubiquitous and consequential as the various social language practices analyzed from a rhetorical perspective.

So, how do I get from the observation that most of us talk to ourselves to the concept of "internal rhetoric"? I coin the term precisely to act as what Kenneth Burke calls a "terministic screen," to call attention to the persuasive or hortatory or sermonic—let's face it, the rhetorical—nature of much thought. "Internal rhetoric" is thus a lens through which to study mental activity rather than a reference to a particular kind of mental activity. By pointing out the rhetorical function of thought rather than positing a separate genre of thought, I accommodate the varieties of internal rhetoric I extrapolate from my primary sources, from deliberate moral reasoning to unconscious molding of self-image.[3]

Why has internal rhetoric not been analyzed by most rhetorical theorists? Perhaps, because the concept is so obvious, because it refers to a practice that is so common—and yet so hard to capture—we ignore its import. Perhaps, because rhetoric has overlapped with pedagogy in significant ways since its inception, we assume that it pays better to teach people how to do (or study) public rhetoric. Perhaps, finally, it is a felt paradox in the concept itself, that "internal rhetoric" is somehow an oxymoronic phrase.

The Paradoxical

That "internal rhetoric" may seem paradoxical to both traditional and postmodern rhetoricians is a testament to the internally suasive power of our accepted categories. Postmodernists might object to the word *internal* as being too individualistic, too focused on interior mental activity that cannot, in their view, be separated from the societal discourses that create it. I use the word *internal* to denote not the origin of the persuasion, however, but merely its scene.[4] Internal rhetoric occurs between one aspect of the self and another (e.g., among reason, emotions, and will, or among ego, superego, and id), no matter how those inner selves are seen to be generated. Thus, particularly in the second half of the book, the inner voices conducting the internal rhetoric are seen as largely socially constructed.

"Internal rhetorics" might also seem paradoxical to traditional rhetoricians, who consider rhetoric to be persuasive language use in the public sphere: the art of the rhetor or politician/orator. Certainly, public—interpersonal, as well as civic—rhetoric constitutes the main field of theorizing and teaching about rhetoric since its early history in Greek culture. I am not trying to deny or deconstruct that history; rather, with Bacon, I am trying "to open and stir the earth a little . . . about the roots of this science" (*De Augmentis* 9:131).

I uncover a parallel thread of rhetoric that I argue has been there all along but has been eclipsed by various political, educational, and philosophical factors that have shaped thinking about language use. The factors submerging internal rhetoric beneath its public counterpart began with rhetoric's earliest formalization into a theorized practice: the "art" of rhetoric was initially developed (in Europe, at least) in response to political reforms in fifth-century-B.C.E. Syracuse, when men needed to speak in political assemblies and law courts; a profitable area of education, then, became training privileged men to amass and exert power through public speaking; Socrates, Plato, and Aristotle later reified the association of rhetoric with public speaking by splitting the formerly unified, sophistic art of *logos* between dialectic, the privileged *technē* (discipline, art) of thinking and philosophy, and rhetoric, the amoral practice of persuasion to belief without knowledge.[5] The cultural bias toward acts of public speaking has thus drawn the attention of rhetoricians to public rhetoric and away from internal, mental acts of rhetoric. Beyond "directing the attention" to internal rhetoric,[6] then, this book also examines some of the reasons why this aspect of rhetoric has been submerged throughout the history of the discipline—why "internal rhetoric" feels paradoxical.

The Complex

Unearthing internal rhetoric at various points in history may underscore its widespread recognition and alleviate the sense of paradox in the term, but doing so also complicates the concept far beyond what common parlance would recognize. As Dorothy Sayers might put it, internal rhetoric will achieve "a high degree of onionisation" by the end of this book.[7] I title this book *Internal Rhetorics* in the plural, then, to emphasize the variety of ways that persuasion has been conceptualized as acting within a person.

Thus, part one gives a historical sampling of how moral reasoning and wisdom have been portrayed as internal rhetoric and thus often used to justify public rhetoric. In chapter 1, I demonstrate that internal rhetoric is portrayed as early in European literature as the *Iliad* and that Isocrates formulates its most classical expression in his encomium on *logos,* rejecting the Platonic split between speech and thought. This rupture, which contributes to the submergence of internal rhetoric in rhetorical studies, is evident both in Plato's various portrayals of rhetoric and the linguistic nature of thought and in Aristotle's failure to connect personal deliberation with rhetoric, which for him refers only to public oratory. Both Plato and Aristotle portray the *psychē* as having multiple parts, however, leading into the crucial role that faculty psychology plays in the next chapter.

In chapter 2, I point out that British Enlightenment figures as diverse as Francis Bacon, Lord Shaftesbury, and Richard Whately portray mental faculties interacting rhetorically with one another, to the evident chagrin of associationists like John Locke. Although they differ in the ways they present the faculties interacting, they agree that these innate faculties have persuasive effects on one another and that internal rhetoric should be cultivated as a form of moral reasoning.

Onto these accounts, part two layers the added complexity of the unconscious and introduces the ongoing product of individual acts of internal rhetoric, the rhetorical self. In chapter 3, I argue that Kenneth Burke and the authors of *The New Rhetoric,* Chaim Perelman and Lucie Olbrechts-Tyteca, develop the implications of a post-Freudian, primary internal rhetoric, which is not always conscious or from conscious sources and which is much more ubiquitous than the cultivated internal rhetoric portrayed in part one. This primary internal rhetoric has appeared in part one, but only as uncultivated internal rhetoric, an immoral expression of the passions when cultivated internal rhetoric is not practiced.

In chapter 4, I argue that George Herbert Mead and Lev Vygotsky provide models for the evolution and development of internal rhetoric. I use their accounts of internalized speech to argue that internal rhetoric is constituted by the social language uses each person is exposed to, and in return constitutes the workings of the mind—and thus, the rhetorical self. Primary internal rhetoric thus takes on another new meaning: it is primary not only to cultivated internal rhetoric but also to the human self as it takes in, processes, and produces language.

In the conclusion, then, I tie together these two major threads—the conscious "art" of cultivated internal rhetoric developed in part one and the unconscious "nature" of primary internal rhetoric posited largely (but not exclusively) in part two. I argue for a version of the rhetorical self that takes into account both the ways we are formed by and formulate internal and external rhetorics and the ways that our physical bodies act as a contributing scene—an agora—for internal rhetoric. Theorizing primary internal rhetoric in this strong, constituent form does not rule out contemporary attention to cultivated internal rhetoric; rather, the rhetorical self necessitates a reformulation of cultivated internal rhetoric as a means of moral reasoning in an era when the capacity of humans for moral agency has been called into question. The final significance of this theory of cultivated and primary internal rhetorics, then, is that it provides a framework for thinking about how complex—and even divided—socially constructed selves have moral agency in an ideologically saturated world.

The Enablers

The quotation from the Martha "Patty" Rogers diary is printed by permission. The diary manuscript is in the Rogers Family Diaries collection of the American Antiquarian Society, Worchester, Massachusetts.

Although the voices in my own head have to take ultimate responsibility for this book, they have been abetted by many mentors, colleagues, and friends over the years. Herman Cohen, Wendall V. Harris, and Jeffrey S. Walker offered cogent criticism when we were all at the Pennsylvania State University. Since then, my friends and colleagues at the University of Massachusetts—Peter Elbow, Anne Herrington, Linda LaDuc, and Charles Moran—have read and commented on parts of the book and been supportive of other aspects of my work. I have also benefited from discussion of the framework of this study with the participants in the Symposium for the Study of Writing and Teaching Writing (UMass, July 2000): Liz Bryant, Blythe Clinchy, Jane Danielewicz, Kate Dionne, Peter Elbow (convener), Donald C. Jones, Irene Papoulis, Erika Scheurer, and Wini Wood. I thank Stephen Clingman and the UMass English Department for providing release time during the 1996–1997 academic year to work on this project.

The pressures of graduate school formed precious friendships for me with Linda Ferreira-Buckley, Rhonda Grego, and Cynthia Miecznikowski Sheard, and those friends have proved diamonds in our subsequent junior faculty days, which I dub "female quixotism" after T. G. Tenney's novel. Other female Quixotes dear to me are Lynnette Leidy Sievert and Beth Rothermel—western Mass is a warmer place for their presence. Not to slight the guys in my life, I thank Steve Brown for keeping me laughing and warm and Sheldon for keeping me walking and covered with dog hair—they have helped me keep my perspective over the last few years.

I also thank Karl Kageff of Southern Illinois University Press for his faith in the project and for his support and sense of humor. Carol

Burns and Elaine Otto were crucial to the final preparation of the manuscript. In addition to thanking the book's anonymous reviewers for their cogent suggestions, I especially thank Gregory Clark for his truly magnanimous review—he is a model of scholarly generosity.

Finally, Marie J. Secor has been a mentor and friend since the beginning of this project. Seven years ago, I thanked Marie for "freely provid[ing] cogent criticism of the text, stimulating intellectual discussion, pedagogical advice and example, and unflagging moral support," and today I am even more in her debt. She is my paradigm for how academia can be a nurturing and yet intellectually rigorous environment, and I try to live up to her example with my own students.

Internal Rhetorics

Introduction

Arguments about how broadly we should define the field of rhetoric have been as integral a part of rhetorical history as arguments about the value of rhetoric vis-à-vis philosophy—and perhaps have the same source: Plato.

> Socrates: Well, then, isn't the rhetorical art, taken as a whole, a way of directing the soul by means of speech, not only in the lawcourts and on other public occasions but also in private? Isn't it one and the same art whether its subject is great or small, and no more to be held in esteem—if it is followed correctly—when its questions are serious than when they are trivial? Or what have you heard about all this?
>
> Phaedrus: Well, certainly not what *you* have! Artful speaking and writing is found mainly in the lawcourts; also perhaps in the Assembly. That's all I've heard. (*Phaedrus* 261a–b)

The scope of rhetoric has been the subject of much scholarly commentary, with such notable metacommentary as Richard Whately arguing that it is useless to argue about the exact boundaries of an abstract concept (*Elements of Rhetoric* 1–2), David Fleming (among others) arguing that all definitions—including those of rhetoric—reflect the interests of those positing them, and Robert L. Scott arguing against the necessity of defining rhetoric at all. Any definition of the scope of rhetoric I could posit here would be begging the question of whether self-persuasion is *really* rhetoric, so I argue instead that a study of internal rhetoric addresses established concerns in both traditionally and expansively defined rhetorical studies and reconstructs them in historically and socially responsible ways.

Traditional definitions of rhetoric focus on rhetoric as an intentional practice and often a specific genre of linguistic action. Rhetoric is seen as an "art," a deliberately cultivated practice and pedagogy often limited to certain genres of overtly persuasive speech and writing, such as Aristotle's deliberative, forensic, and epideictic oratory. This limitation of rhetoric to common civic practices is seen as historically validated. George Kennedy, for example, opens *A New History of Classical Rhetoric* with this statement: "This book is a revised history of rhetoric as that term was usually understood throughout classical antiquity: the art of persuasion by words or the art of civic discourse, taught and practiced in schools and applied in public address" (xi). Certainly, if we define rhetoric as only having to do with public address, internal rhetoric is an unwarranted expansion of the term *rhetoric,* except for the few discussions of preparation for public rhetoric being internally persuasive (e.g., Isocrates, Blair).

On the other end of the spectrum of rhetorical studies are those who see all human meaning-making as rhetorical. The expansive definition of rhetoric is exemplified by this statement on the part of the National Developmental Project on Rhetoric's Committee on the Scope of Rhetoric:

> Rhetorical studies are properly concerned with the process by which symbols and systems of symbols have influence on beliefs, values, attitudes, and actions, and they embrace all forms of human communication, not exclusively public address nor communication within any one class or cultural group. (Bitzer and Black 208)

Expansive rhetoric thus encompasses the extent to which language permeates and influences human lives—and, having used Kennedy's definition of traditional rhetoric earlier, it is only fair for me to mention that he discusses rhetoric as a "universal phenomenon, one found even among animals" in *Comparative Rhetorics* (3). In terms of the analysis I presented in the preface, expansive rhetoric looks at the rhetorical *function* of all language and symbol use rather than rhetoric as a specific *genre* of discourse.

Advocates of expansive rhetoric downplay rhetoric as a learned, deliberate art that focuses on the intentional actions of the rhetor, and they concentrate on the rhetorical effect of all kinds of symbol use on (usually) human behavior and attitude. They thus focus on people as *audience* for rhetoric rather than individuals as *producers* of rhetoric. While rhetoricians tend not to go to the extremes of postmodernism and deny the individual rhetor any agency, expansive rhetorics embed intentional rhetoric in a context of pervasive "rhetoricality" as characterized by John Bender and David Wellbery:

> *Modernism is an age not of rhetoric, but of rhetoricality,* the age, that is, of a generalized rhetoric that penetrates to the deepest levels of human experience. . . . [Rhetoricality] manifests the groundless, infinitely ramifying characteristics of discourse in the modern world. For this reason, it allows for no explanatory metadiscourse that is not already itself rhetorical. Rhetoric is no longer the title of a doctrine and a practice, nor a form of cultural memory; it becomes instead something like the condition of our existence. (25; emphasis in original)

While I and many others would quarrel with their claim that rhetoric no longer applies to the traditional definition I described above, their distinction between rhetoric and rhetoricality is a useful way to think about traditional and expansive rhetorics. In a sense, rhetoric has come full circle in its expansive manifestation: the broader sophistic concern with all of *logos* (language, speech, reasoning, thought) that was codified into the art of persuasive speaking and writing is now being broadened again to cover the contemporary equivalent of *logos:* a concern with how language in all of its manifestations influences humans (and sometimes other sentient beings).

Surely no one holding an expansivist perspective on rhetoric would have any quarrel with including internal rhetoric, although persuasion of the self has not been treated with any particular attention in specifically rhetorical terms. But I want to argue that internal rhetoric in one form or another works within both traditional and expansive rhetorics. To do so, I return to the distinction between cultivated and primary internal rhetorics that I sketched, but did not fully develop, in the preface.

As I noted earlier, Kennedy argues that classical rhetoricians usually understand rhetoric in the context of public address. In this book, I focus on the exceptions to that "usually" as a corrective to accounts of rhetoric that discuss only interpersonal discourse. Part one of this book thus gives historical precedents for including the persuasion we do inside our heads under the rubric of rhetoric: it has often been compared with public rhetoric and seen as a cultivated art, using language in ethical or unethical ways to make decisions or to incite desired actions or attitudes in the self. In its most deliberate manifestations, internal rhetoric can be included in the *art* of rhetoric insofar as it is characterized by intentional (self-)persuasion toward a desired end and insofar as it is a learned and often deliberately cultivated behavior. Examples may be found in guided meditation or deliberately constructive self-talk or visualization, but also in the more common process of reasoning through choices and dilemmas presented to us on a daily basis. Whether they are aware of it or not, coaches, spiritual leaders, and therapists are all practitioners of *rhetorica docens,* to the extent that they teach people to use self-talk toward certain ends. Reflecting the intentionally persuasive nature of this kind of internal rhetoric, I argue that the study of cultivated internal rhetoric is a warranted extension of even the traditional definition of rhetoric.

If cultivated internal rhetoric correlates with traditional understandings of rhetoric, primary internal rhetoric fits even more easily under the rubric of expansive rhetorics. That is, just as people can intentionally influence their behavior or attitudes through self-persuasion, they do so unconsciously as well—and the same pervasive uses of language that are studied in expansive rhetorics can also be found within the psyche and studied as primary internal rhetoric.[1] By distinguishing cultivated from primary internal rhetoric, I want to imply not two distinct genres of internal rhetoric but rather the poles of a spectrum of intentionality and consciousness with which people use internal rhetoric. Thus, a writer trying to decide whether to approach her next sentence one way or another—or to take a break and eat chocolate—will almost certainly be practicing internal rhetoric at "varying degrees of deliberateness and unawareness" (Burke, *A Rhetoric* 35).

This study of internal rhetoric does more than just make explicit a group of rhetorical phenomena already implicit in expansive rhetorics. In addition, it creates a bridge between traditional rhetoric's attention to people as rhetors and expansive rhetoric's attention to people as audience. Internal rhetoric focuses on the divided nature of people as rhetors: We are no longer black boxes either producing or receiving discourse, but complex agents that take in cultural and direct rhetorics; reject, manipulate, or swallow them whole; and re-create or respond to them in personal utterances and actions, intentional or not. Reject, manipulate, swallow whole: these are simplifications of the complex rhetorical negotiations that take place within people as we receive and produce discourse. Thus, we do not need to mothball traditional rhetorics to extend the field of rhetoric to internal and expansive models. The terminologies developed over centuries of rhetorical tradition can be usefully applied to a broader range of discursive practices than those for which they were originally developed, including the rhetoric that goes on in our own heads.

In calling attention to self-persuasion, this study also addresses a much more long-standing fissure than that between traditional and expansive rhetorics. Ever since Plato questioned the epistemological and ethical standing of rhetoric, philosophy has seen itself as antirhetoric: the esoteric search for timeless truths and values instead of the public construction of knowledge and principles in response to occasions for action. Internal rhetoric pushes the philosophical edge of rhetoric by foregrounding the rhetorical component of all decision making and, consequently, of our sense of "self." Whether knowledge and values are seen as foundational or constructed, internal rhetoric helps explain how we act and are acted upon in the shifting contexts of our lives.

Part One

Internal Rhetoric in History: Perspectives on Moral Reasoning

The internal rhetorics I develop here are based on psychologies that see the mind as functionally articulated into such innate powers as Reason, the Imagination, the Will, and the Emotions. In chapter 1, I begin with the internal rhetoric portrayed in the *Iliad* to establish how ancient is the idea that people persuade themselves into certain decisions or actions. I use Isocrates' arguments about the unity of *logos* to place internal rhetoric firmly within the scope of rhetorical studies, and then I show how Plato and Aristotle's attempts to isolate *logos* as thought from *logos* as speech fail to account for some of their own psychological assumptions.

Chapter 2 focuses on philosophers and rhetoricians who see rhetoric as taking place in the mind to reconcile dissonances among the mental faculties. Francis Bacon, the first philosopher to describe rhetoric as being intrapersonal, argues that internal rhetoric is necessary to enable ethical decisions and actions. The third earl of Shaftesbury, although agreeing with Plato that reason is naturally dominant in the psyche, sees cultivated internal rhetoric as necessary to overcome the illicit persuasions of the appetites, while Richard Whately argues that internal rhetoric is necessary at times to raise proper emotions, not just to quash improper ones. These portrayals of internal rhetoric take place in a context of a masculinist society whose assumptions about the gendering of the faculties are called into question by Mary Astell and Mary Wollstonecraft. Furthermore, they stand against associationist psychologies like that of John Locke, which are more concerned with the role of the faculties in responding to external stimuli than using faculty psychology to explain and alleviate mental dissonances.

All these philosophers have different explanations for which faculty tends to dominate others in moral decision making, but they might all agree that the issue is central to the conduct of our day-to-day lives.

1

Classical Variations on Internal Rhetoric

And my city,
its towers and sacred places of the Gods,
of these I robbed my miserable self
when I commanded all to drive *him* out,
the criminal since proved by God impure
and of the race of Laius.
To this guilt I bore witness against myself.

—Sophocles, *Oedipus the King*

Rhetoric—the word, the practice, and the study and theorization of—emerges in ancient Greece as the art of the (public) speaker, so it may seem willfully perverse to insist on a branch of the classical rhetorical art that occurs within the mind. Yet from the earliest sources in which public rhetoric is depicted, self-persuasion is also portrayed, and it is only after Plato splits *logos* between rhetoric, the art of public speech, and philosophy, the art of thought (which he still characterizes as mental conversation) that the internal aspect of rhetoric gets submerged. Isocrates, on the other hand, asserts an identity between public rhetoric and the kind of private deliberation I call internal rhetoric. Because his rhetorical treatment of deliberation provides exactly the kind of opening into the study of internal rhetoric this history requires, I re-create a classical internal rhetoric constructed around the writings of Isocrates to analyze how and why Plato and Aristotle limit rhetoric to the public sphere.[1] Isocrates is receiving fresh attention from rhetorical scholars, and my account of his claims for the private benefits of rhetoric balances their focus on civic discourse, adding up to the more holistic view of *logos* that Isocrates espouses.

This history of internal rhetoric does not begin with Isocrates, however. By the time he writes, Isocrates can already assume both that his audience is familiar with the metaphor of thought as an internal dialogue and that they perceive this internal rhetoric as a good thing, a goal to work towards. How far back can this assumption of the positive value of internal rhetoric be traced? A natural place to look is in the earliest extant major Greek text, the *Iliad.*

The Internal Rhetoric of Heroes in the Iliad

Many histories of ancient Greek rhetoric begin with the "traditional" rhetoric exemplified in the *Iliad,*[2] cited for its abundance of rhetorical action: Gods, heroes, and others (including horses) plead with, cajole, taunt, incite, command, and propitiate each other throughout the more physical action of the epic.[3] Richard Enos, for example, discusses Homeric rhetoric as part of his argument that rhetoric emerged as a discipline over a long period of time, not just in fifth-century Greece (ix). For Enos, Homeric rhetoric illustrates a growing consciousness about thought and language and a concomitant "shift from a theocentric notion to more of an anthropocentric notion of discourse" (5). Susan Jarratt delves into the "rhetorical moments of the epic" to critique the theory that preliterate "forms of consciousness" were incapable of "elaborated syllogistic logic and the introspection or critical distance presumed necessary for such logic" (*Rereading the Sophists* 35, 31). She argues instead that "mythic discourse is capable of containing the beginnings of a 'rhetorical consciousness.' . . . The consciousness expresses itself both through public argument and internal debate" (35).[4] Jarratt takes issue with Bruno Snell's assertion that "there is in Homer no genuine reflexion, no dialogue of the soul with itself" (Snell 19) in order to assert that there is no radical split between the mythic consciousness portrayed in the *Iliad* and the rational consciousness portrayed, paradigmatically, by Plato.

What is implied, but not stated, in Jarratt's argument is the oddness of Snell's conclusion that "there are no divided feelings in Homer" (19) after he has argued strongly that the archaic Greeks perceived different mental activities as arising from distinct entities that have the properties of both physical organs and abstract powers or functions. According to Snell, their perceptions of what we would term body and mind are each more indicative of a collection of powers than a unified individual.[5] Because the various mental faculties are perceived as distinct entities rather than parts of a psychic whole, Snell concludes, "Two different things or substances engage in a quarrel with one another"—which he does not consider reflecting mental activity (19). I agree with Jarratt in drawing a different conclusion than Snell from Homer's depiction of articulated mental powers: that the mental divisiveness portrayed in Homer necessarily constitutes what James J. Murphy calls the "rhetorical consciousness" and what I call internal rhetoric. I thus begin my history of internal rhetoric with a closer look at these same instances of the heroes talking to themselves rather than to their comrades and the gods.[6]

That these three audiences are distinct in Homer is evident in the first instance of internal rhetoric portrayed, after Agamemnon threatens to take Briseis from Achilleus:

> And the anger came on Peleus' son [Achilleus], and within
> his shaggy breast *the heart was divided two ways,* pondering
> whether to draw from beside his thigh the sharp sword . . .
> or else to check the spleen within and keep down his anger.
> *Now as he weighed in mind and spirit* these two courses
> and was drawing from its scabbard the great sword,
> Athene descended from the sky.
>
> (1:188–95; emphasis added)[7]

Clearly, Homer is depicting a debate internal to Achilleus, introduced as his heart being torn [*diandicha mermērixen,* to halt between two opinions] and then summarized as a dialogue *[hormainō]* between mind *[phrēn]* and spirit *[thumos].* Each of the instances of internal rhetoric are demarcated similarly, and this clear insistence on mental strife, parallel to interpersonal and physical strife, seems to belie Snell's assertion that in Homer such mental organs are motivationally inert: "The *thymos* and the *noos* are so very little different from other physical organs that they cannot very well be looked upon as a genuine source of impulses. . . . Mental and spiritual acts are due to the impact of exterior factors" (20). The discussion taking place within Achilleus's breast may be instigated by his argument with Agamemnon, but it is clearly demarcated from his interactions with both Agamemnon and Athena. While the intervention of Athena in this case seems to support Snell's contention that "Homer does not know genuine personal decisions; even where a hero is shown pondering two alternatives the intervention of the gods plays the key role" (20), the subsequent instances of internal rhetoric do not get resolved in the same way.

Odysseus's internal rhetoric shows a more typical isolation of internal rhetoric from rhetoric addressed to others and to the gods. Odysseus, like the other heroes, talks to himself when he is in a tight spot in the midst of battle:

> Now Odysseus the spear-famed was left alone, nor did any
> of the Argives stay beside him, since fear had taken all of them.
> And troubled, *he spoke then to his own great-hearted spirit:*
> "Ah me, what will become of me? It will be a great evil
> if I run, fearing their multitude, yet deadlier if I am caught
> alone; and Kronos' son drove to flight the rest of the Danaans.
> Yet still, *why does the heart within me debate on these things?*
> Since I know that it is the cowards who walk out of the fighting,
> but if one is to win honour in battle, he must by all means
> stand his ground strongly, whether he be struck or strike
> down another."
> *While he was pondering these things in his heart and his spirit*
> the ranks of the armoured Trojans came on against him.
>
> (11:401–12, emphasis added)

This passage is characteristic of the scenes in which heroes talk to themselves in several ways. The language describing the internal rhetoric is formulaic, so the following observations hold for each instance.

Odysseus is portrayed first as speaking [*eipon,* to address] to his valor [*megalētor thumos,* high-minded soul or spirit]. In the midst of the soliloquy, he questions why his *thumos* is conducting a dialogue *[dialegō]*[8] with (or talking back to) him. As in the previous passage discussed, the debate *[hormainō]* is summed up as being between "his heart and his spirit."[9] "Heart" here translates *phrēn,* an organ or faculty located around the physical heart that was the seat of passions.[10] The *thumos* (here, "spirit") is the source of "motion or agitation," the organ that impassions feelings and actions (Snell 9). The crucial difference between this more typical passage and the first scene with Achilleus is that a god does not step in to resolve the internal debate. Rather, Odysseus gives cultural meaning to a biological fight-or-flight reaction—cowards flee, heroes fight—and makes his decision based on those values.

The situation in which Odysseus encourages himself is common to four of the scenes in which characters engage in internal rhetoric—those involving Odysseus, Menelaos, Agenor, and Hector. The heroes are alone, surrounded by the enemy (or facing the vengeful Achilleus, which is just as bad) in the midst of a raging battle, and thus have no one else to trade encouragements with. In desperate circumstances, then, the heroes deliberate whether to run (this way or that), retreat, or fight, and the possible consequences of each action.

At the same time, the reasoning processes and outcomes differ among the heroes. Agenor, for example, weighs his possibilities for survival if he flees either with the rest of the Trojans or goes alone to the river to hide until dark. It is hard to say whether he persuades himself more by noting the futility of these options or their ignominy, but like Odysseus he decides that his best choice of action is to stay and fight. Menelaos, however, finds a cultural premise that competes with the "heroic imperative" (Fenik 71), and so he can justify retreating from a fight:

> "When a man, in the face of divinity, would fight with another
> whom some god honours, the big disaster rolls sudden upon him.
> Therefore, let no Danaan seeing it hold it against me
> if I give way before Hektor, who fights from God."
>
> (17.98-101)

In this soliloquy, Menelaos balances the shamefulness of abandoning the body of a slain leader against the futility of fighting a man favored by the gods. His resolution—to return to the defense of Patroklos's body after finding Aias to help him—reflects the compromise necessary to fulfill both cultural expectations.[11] Hector, like Odysseus and Agenor, imagines the shame that would come to him if he fled and so decides to fight (22.99-130), but unlike either he flees after a trembling *(tromos)* overcomes him (22.136). Thus, while these cases of internal rhetoric described so far occur in similar circumstances, they vary in both the reasoning process used by the protagonist and the decisions arrived at. Bernard Fenik even argues that the "monologues" of the four heroes are so different that "each of the scenes contributes a portrait" individualizing its speaker (6).[12]

Like the first scene portraying Achilleus deliberating, the later instances in which Achilleus talks to his *thumos* are different from the battle monologues sketched above. In none of these latter three cases is he deciding what to do in the midst of battle; instead, he is trying to understand what is happening around him. At the beginning of book 18 he anticipates the news of Patroklos's death by the rout of the Greeks (18.5–16); in book 20, after Achilleus has rejoined the battle, he ponders what happened when Poseidon blurred his vision to remove Aeneas from battle with him (20.344–53); and in book 21, he exclaims upon seeing Lykaon, one of Priam's sons, whom he had previously sold into slavery (21.53–65).[13] In the first two instances, Achilleus reasons from the unknown to a correct surmise of what must have happened. When he sees Lykaon, however, Achilleus seems to be engaging in rather gratuitous metaphor-making:

> "Can this be? Here is a strange thing that my eyes look on.
> Now the great-hearted Trojans, even those I have killed already,
> will stand and rise up again out of the gloom and the darkness
> as this man has come back and escaped the day without pity
> though he was sold into sacred Lemnos; but the main of the grey sea
> could not hold him, though it holds back many who are unwilling."
> (21.54–59)

Achilleus likens the return of Lykaon from slavery in Lemnos to the resurrection of the dead, the sea to the river Styx. Like the previous instances of internal rhetoric during battle, this one results in a decision on a course of action—but through metaphorical rather than deductive or inductive reasoning:

> "But come now, he must be given a taste of our spearhead
> so that I may know inside my heart and make certain
> whether he will come back even from there, or the prospering
> earth will hold him, she who holds back even the strong man."
> (21.60–63)

Achilleus does not need to decide what to do in this situation, since he has sworn to avenge Patroklos's death, but he does pause, in his surprise at seeing Lykaon, to strengthen that resolve—and to convince himself that he is indeed seeing whom he thinks he is seeing—through internal rhetoric.

The *Iliad* thus portrays internal rhetoric in a variety of circumstances and with a variety of types of reasoning, all pointing toward initiating action at a crucial moment. The impetus to talk with oneself comes not only in an argument or a desperate battle situation, but also in situations in which the protagonist needs to clarify his understanding of events.[14] Because of this situational variability, the process of internal rhetoric is not just a weighing of alternatives or an application of cultural imperatives to immediate situations, as the scenes described earlier depict, but may consist of other kinds of reasoning as well. In identifying an instance of recorded thought as internal rhetoric, we must look at the function of the mental action for the individual rather than for genre-specific characteristics. One of the crucial contributions that the *Iliad* makes to a historicized concept of internal rhetoric, then, is that in the use of mental language to initiate considered action, there is no functional difference between "persuasion" and "clarification."

In the archaic Greek society represented by the *Iliad,* the characteristics of internal rhetoric are determined by the perceived concreteness of mental processes.[15] Perhaps because of this articulated, collective view of human faculties, the activity of internal rhetoric does not conflict with physical activity: The mental "organs" contribute to the actions of the rest of the body by clarifying situations, making decisions, and reinforcing convictions. By doing so, the use of internal rhetoric ensures that the activity subsequently embarked upon is the best that can be done in the situation. Thus, internal rhetoric is associated with *aretē* (loosely, virtue) in at least a demonstrative relationship: If it is not a necessary or sufficient characteristic of action in accordance with *aretē,* then it at least is used rhetorically in the epic to delineate the reasoning behind heroic actions.

This final observation about internal rhetoric in some way being associated with *aretē* leads to the question of whether it is peculiar to the warrior's *aretē* portrayed in the *Iliad* or perhaps also characteristic of other varieties of *aretē.* Alasdair MacIntyre argues that *aretē* is relative to the function a person plays in society: "A man who performs his socially allotted function possesses *[aretē].* The *[aretē]* of one function or role is quite different from that of another. The *[aretē]* of a king lies in ability to command, of a warrior in courage, of a wife in fidelity, and so on" (8).[16] I have not found any portrayals of internal rhetoric contributing to the *aretē* of social classes other than the *aristoi.* Although a number of moral precepts for farmers are to be found in Hesiod's *Works and Days,* the value of talking to oneself is not one of them, and the lists of renowned women in *The Catalogues of Women* and *The Eoiae* do little more than record who gave birth to whom.[17] For this historical layer of meaning of internal rhetoric, given the evidence at hand, I must provisionally conclude that internal rhetoric is a means by which the *aristoi* reinforce their *aretē* and leave the question of universal application open.[18]

The *Iliad* gives us a clear picture of internal rhetoric as early as archaic Greek culture. Given this context, the rest of the chapter takes up the question that occupies the bulk of this book: What is the relationship between the "art" of rhetoric, described so thoroughly and variously in pedagogical and theoretical texts since the fourth century B.C.E., and internal rhetoric? I continue tracing the thread of internal rhetoric in discourses of a more explicitly rhetorical and philosophical nature. As I indicated earlier, the main theoretical source for a classical picture of internal rhetoric is Isocrates. Keeping in mind that Isocrates has a tradition stretching back at least to the *Iliad* of people persuading themselves as well as others, I argue in the following section that internal rhetoric is Isocrates' primary tool for training citizen-orators—as well as for justifying his own pedagogical enterprise.

Isocrates on the Indivisibility of Logos

Isocrates argues that the proper goal of education is the ability "to govern wisely both our own households and the commonwealth" (*Antidosis* §285).[19] Contemporary scholars have focused exclusively on the latter, political aspect of Isocratean education and writings, which is no doubt the ultimate goal of his teaching. Takis Poulakos, for example, argues that Isocrates' rhetorical agenda was to re-create a "unified polis" through the "unequivocal interdependence between citizenry and citizen" (105). Yun Lee Too has a different reading, arguing that Isocrates "shows us how an individual, above all a writer, can invoke and comply with a dominant cultural language, namely that of democracy, but at the same time also subvert and question it" (234). Both scholars focus on the public uses and implications of Isocrates' rhetorical teaching, practice, and philosophy, and both cite the paradigmatic expression of this civic-mindedness in Isocrates' "hymn to logos":[20]

> Because there has been implanted in us the power to persuade *[peithō]* each other and to make clear *[dēloō]* to each other whatever we desire, not only have we escaped the life of wild beasts, but we have come together and founded cities and made laws and invented arts;

> and, generally speaking, there is no institution devised by man which the power of speech *[logos]* has not helped us to establish. (*Nicocles* §§5–7)[21]

Clearly, civic rhetoric is an important venue for both Isocrates and those who would understand his writings.

Without denying the central role that civic life and rhetoric has for Isocrates, I focus here on Isocrates' first locus of educational responsibility—the ability to "govern wisely . . . our own households" *(idioi oikoi),* a more private aspect of Isocratean teaching and concern. The connection he draws here is not just between domestic and political business, but between the private and public benefits of language use *(logos).* In this section, I argue that Isocrates' interest in personal *logos* is not just a stylistic antithesis or an unexamined counterpart to his primary interest in civic affairs and rhetoric, but a fully developed philosophy that is crucial to his project to promote and teach civic virtue and responsible public rhetoric.

Terminology in this section presents a bit of a problem, because we are so used to following Plato's definition of philosophy and Aristotle's of rhetoric.[22] Isocrates' definition of philosophy is very different from Plato's, and he does not use the term *rhetoric* at all. The aim of Isocratean philosophy is closer to Aristotle's definition of *phronēsis,* practical wisdom, than to the Platonic/Aristotelean goal of *epistēmē,* knowledge of universal truths. In his language arts teaching, Isocrates uses the broad term *logos,* referring to language ability and use in both thought and speech. These were not eccentric usages in his time, because both *philosophy* and *rhetoric* were neologisms, the definitions of which had not yet solidified.[23] Given these considerations, I will continue to use *internal rhetoric* for the broadly rhetorical function of thought sketched in the preface and limned further in the previous section. Even though the term is not Isocratean, it illuminates Isocrates' concern with private, ethical, and epistemological language use.

Isocrates elaborates on his view of the private benefits of *logos* by explicating how it affects our day-to-day lives:

> It is by this also that we confute the bad and extol the good. Through this we educate the ignorant and appraise the wise; for the power to speak well is taken as the surest index *[sēmeion]* of a sound understanding, and discourse which is true and lawful and just is the outward image *[eidōlon]* of a good and faithful soul. (*Nicocles* §7)

Isocrates thus sees his *logon paideia* as applying not only to the elite men who participate in Athenian democracy but to people in any area of life in which individuals interact with one another. This is his first formulation of the intimate connection between the understanding *(phronis)* or soul *(psychē)* and the power of speech *(logos)*: he calls the latter a *sēmeion,* a sign or token of the former; and moreover he writes as though this relationship is one accepted by his audience.[24] In fact, Isocrates goes on to assert that *logos* is indivisible, implying that the Platonic bifurcation of thought and speech has no practical purpose. Isocrates is responding, if not to a specific Platonic dialogue like the *Gorgias,* then to the same intellectual milieu in which Plato separates rhetoric (as persuasive speech) from dialectic (as truth-seeking thought). He is more interested in synthesis than analysis.[25]

Isocrates has already rejected one common division of *logos* in his hymn to *logos:* that "the power to persuade" *(peithō)* is different from the power "to make clear to" *(dēloō)* each other, a division that encourages the separation of rhetoric (persuasion) from other aspects of *logos* (thinking, reasoning, logic). In preserving the unity of persuasion and clarification, Isocrates echoes their functional similarity in the internal rhetoric portrayed in the *Iliad,* in which both are used as impetuses for action. His arguments about the contiguity of speech and thought, rhetoric and meaning-making, are made explicit in a series of three parallel claims about the identity of rhetorical speech and thought:

> With this faculty *[logos]* we both contend against others on matters which are open to dispute and seek light for ourselves on things which are unknown; for the same arguments which we use in persuading others when we speak in public, we employ also when we deliberate in our own thoughts; and while we call eloquent those who are able to speak before a crowd, we regard as sage those who most skillfully debate their problems in their own minds. (*Nicocles* §8)

Isocrates here makes three comparisons between public rhetoric and thought as manifestations of *logos*. First, he argues that *logos* comprehends a range of human activities from contention over public issues *(agōnizimai)* to the private act of seeking to understand *(skeptomai)* the unknown. The almost antithetical nature of this comparison is seen in the two verbs used for the activities: The first is related to struggle and contention, and the second to seeing, beholding, contemplating. In this clause he does not yet equate the two linguistic activities, but emphasizes that they share the essential nature of *logos*.

He draws a stronger connection between thought and rhetoric in the second clause, where he claims that we use the same proofs *(pisteis)* to persuade others *(peithō)* that we use in private deliberation *(bouleuō)*. This claim seems pretty straightforward at first: We use the same reasoning whether we are speaking or thinking. Not only is the reasoning the same, however; the medium in which it occurs is the same, because in this assertion, Isocrates begins to emphasize the linguistic nature of thought. In the first analogy, the word Isocrates uses on the "thought" side of the parallelisms, *skeptomai*, employs a visual metaphor similar to the English use of "to seek light" or "to see" for "to think." But in this second clause Isocrates switches to linguistically based terms for thought: His second term for "think" *(bouleuō)*, like our verb "to deliberate," might be used for either thought or discussions addressed to an external audience. Isocrates brings thought and speech together not just as an analogy but as a synthesis of both terms under the rubric of *logos*.

Isocrates' final parallel between thought and speech ties together several of the arguments developed in this section. Because of the unified nature of *logos*, calling people eloquent *(rhētorikos)* is equivalent to calling them prudent or well counseled *(euboulos)*, since the sage are those who best converse with themselves *(autous arista . . . dialechthōsin)*. This final description of thought as a conversation or debate with oneself concludes the transition from thought as an unaddressed, visual activity of the *psychē* to thought as an addressed linguistic transaction, a *dialogos*.[26] Moreover, the rhetorical nature of this linguistic interaction is implied in the adjective *euboulos*, which indicates the successful completion of a rhetorical act, one of counseling.[27]

In his defense of rhetoric, then, Isocrates draws together thought and rhetoric under the rubric of *logos* by emphasizing the linguistic, rhetorical nature of thought. To bring out the linguistic aspect of thought, he uses verbs associated with interpersonal language use *(bouleuō, dialegomai)*, but uses them reflexively to underscore the idea that thought is an internalized use of the same *logos* that rhetors use publicly. This reflexive use of dialogical verbs implies vestiges of the divided sense of self that was so concretized in Homeric internal rhetoric.[28] In this passage on internal rhetoric, however, the inner divisions implied by the use of the reflexive pronoun with a dialogical verb are more ambiguous than the Homeric formula in which people speak to their own *thumoi*. But for Isocrates, as for Homer, this inward rhetoric has both a positive ethical evaluation in its own right and a role as the source of ethical behavior.

In the final comparison between thought and rhetoric, Isocrates makes the positive ethical evaluation that forms the basis of his entire defense of rhetoric. His juxtaposition of *rhētorikos* and *euboulos* suggests that he places speech and thought on the same scale of values, in which the skill of the best *(aristos)* language users may equally be called eloquence or sagacity. Isocrates' last observation about the valuative equivalence of eloquence and sagacity places his arguments about *logos* firmly within the rubric of philosophy. This positive reevaluation of *rhētorikos* has been carefully built up from Isocrates' hymn to *logos,* through these specific claims for the power and uses of *logos,* and it culminates in this sweeping pronouncement:

> And, if there is need to speak in brief summary of this power *[dynamis]*, we shall find that none of the things which are done with intelligence *[phronimos]* take place without the help of speech *[alogos]*, but that in all our actions as well as in all our thoughts speech *[logos]* is our guide, and is most employed by those who have the most wisdom *[noos]*. *(Nicocles* §9)

Logos guides all human actions and thoughts, and is used the most by the most "mindful" people.[29] This passage, taken in connection with that immediately preceding it—"we regard as sage those who most skillfully debate their problems in their own minds" *(Nicocles* §9)—suggests that there is a causal connection between internal rhetoric and ethical, wise behavior for Isocrates. In fact, internal rhetoric is the cornerstone in Isocrates' ideal of the philosophical life. For Isocrates, as for Homer, *aretē* and philosophy are not divorced from the active life, but ensure that actions taken are the best possible in any given circumstance. To show how internal rhetoric enables ethical behavior, I turn now to two other key aspects of Isocratean theory, his key term *kairos* and his discussion of the education of an orator.

One of Isocrates' primary contributions as a rhetorician, philosopher, and educator is his insistence on the centrality of *kairos*—that sense of due measure or fitness or, since he most frequently uses it in relation to time, the proper or critical time.[30] Isocrates uses *kairos* in many ways, such as to point out the political or ethical appropriateness of an action ("Do not think that getting is gain or spending is loss; for neither one nor the other has the same significance at all times, but either, when done in season *[en kairō]* and with honor, benefits the doer" [*Nicocles* §50]) or to maintain the fiction of oral delivery in his addresses ("Now I am not going to quote from it [*Against the Sophists*] my criticisms of others; for they are too long for the present occasion *[kairos]*" [§194]).[31] The most important use Isocrates has for *kairos,* however, is as a definitive concept in both his teaching of rhetoric and his understanding of wisdom and philosophy. Given my earlier argument that Isocrates equates eloquence with wisdom, these are not two separate concerns but rather method and goal in the same enterprise.

In his early work, *Against the Sophists,* Isocrates criticizes other teachers of rhetoric for claiming to teach rhetorical commonplaces as if they were alphabetic building blocks for speeches. This plug-in approach to instruction is useless for rhetoric, because "what has been said by one speaker is not equally useful for the speaker who comes after him" (§12). Instead, Isocrates argues that "oratory is good only if it has the qualities of fitness for the occasion *[kairos]*, propriety of style *[prepontōs]*, and originality of treatment *[to kairos]*" (§13). He claims that having a "knowledge *[epistēmē]* of the elements out of which we make and compose all discourses" (§16) is less difficult than having the judgment to use them:

> But to choose from these elements those which should be employed for each subject, to join them together, to arrange them properly, and also, not to miss what the occasion *[kairos]* demands but appropriately to adorn the whole speech with striking thoughts *[enthymēmata]* and to clothe it in flowing and melodious phrase—these things, I hold, require much study and are the task of a vigorous and imaginative mind *[psychē andrikos kai doxastikos]*. (§§16–17)

Success in achieving this kind of judgment requires a propitious confluence of aptitude and practice on the part of the student and knowledge and experience on the part of the teacher. As difficult as this accomplishment appears, the ability to grasp and use *kairos* is a key factor in an orator's success.

How, then, does Isocrates propose to teach this understanding of *kairos*? Since we do not have the complete text of *Against the Sophists,*[32] I turn again to the *Antidosis* to outline the educational methods and objectives for teaching a grasp of *kairos.* In keeping with his high standards for rhetors cited above, Isocrates' demands on both teachers and students are stringent:

> The teachers of philosophy impart all the forms of discourse in which the mind expresses itself. Then, when they have made them familiar and thoroughly conversant with these lessons, they set them at exercises, habituate them to work, and require them to combine in practice the particular things which they have learned, in order that they may grasp them more firmly and bring their theories *[doxai]* into closer touch with the occasions *[kairoi]* for applying them. (*Antidosis* §§183–84)

Thus only practice—one of the three requisites for rhetorical training (along with aptitude and knowledge)—helps the student orator become adept at *kairos,* because there are no set rules for when any rhetorical device will be appropriate or effective.

In a continuation of the above passage, Isocrates reinforces the necessity of kairotic awareness by insisting on the relative nature of human affairs:

> —I say "theories," for no system of knowledge can possibly cover these occasions, since in all cases they elude our science *[epistēmē].* Yet those who most apply their minds to them and are able to discern the consequences which for the most part grow out of them, will most often meet these occasions in the right way. (*Antidosis* §184)

Isocrates' distinction between *doxa* and *epistēmē* differs from Plato's, the usual point of reference for this question. Plato argues that true knowledge *(epistēmē)* is possible through dialectic, and that *doxai* are merely fallible human opinions open to manipulation through rhetoric.[33] For Isocrates, the realm of rhetoric is the world of human affairs, in which we can have no certain knowledge—thus *doxai* are "working theor[ies] based on practical experience" (2:290n. a) and *epistēmē* is impossible in this area. This uncertainty in human affairs makes an ability to grasp *kairos* important and an education providing this ability—which Isocrates claims to provide—doubly so.

Despite the difficulties of mastering *kairos,* Isocrates does claim here that it can be done by "those who most apply their minds" to rhetorical occasions. Because Isocrates has argued elsewhere that "foreknowledge of future events is not vouchsafed to our human nature" (*Against the Sophists* §1) and here that "no system of knowledge can possibly cover these occasions," he must explain the ability of people to know enough to act effectively in uncertain situations. Not everyone has this ability, according to Isocrates; rather, he sees it as characteristic of wise people.

> For since it is not in the nature of man to attain a science by the possession of which we can know positively what we should do or what we should say, in the next resort I hold that man to be wise *[sophos]* who is able by his powers of conjecture *[doxai]* to arrive generally at the best course, and I hold that man to be a philosopher *[philosophos]* who occupies himself with the studies from which he will most quickly gain that kind of insight. (*Antidosis* §271)

If the wise are described here as those who can arrive at the best course of action by developing working theories, I have shown previously that they are also those who "most skillfully debate their problems in their own minds" (*Nicocles* §8). I conclude, then, that Isocrates shows how wise people develop their working theories and contingency plans by the process I have labeled internal rhetoric. By talking through problems with themselves, wise people are able to grasp the *kairos* of any situation and consequently take the best possible course of action.

This reading of *kairos* and internal rhetoric is reinforced by another comment Isocrates makes in *To Nicocles:* "The well-educated man must, as the result of his training in whatever discipline, show ability to deliberate and decide *[bouleuō]*" (§51).[34] As I have previously discussed, the dialogical implications of the verb *bouleuō* lend themselves to a rhetorical view of such deliberations. Isocrates is also concerned in this oration (as he is in the hymn to *logos* discussed above) with the ability to judge wisdom in another person, advising that one should take "careful note of them when they present their views on particular situations *[kairoi]*" (*To Nicocles* §52).[35] Thus Isocrates measures wisdom in people by the quality of their internal rhetoric as demonstrated by the appropriateness of their actions and opinions in particular situations.

This is precisely the goal of education for Isocrates, a practical wisdom that allows people to debate in their own minds—practice internal rhetoric—and arrive at the best action possible in an uncertain world. He thus considers educated people "those who manage well the circumstances which they encounter day by day, and who possess a judgment which is accurate in meeting occasions *[kairoi]* as they arise and rarely misses the expedient course of action" (*Panathenaicus* §30). This association of internal rhetoric, *kairos,* and wisdom is crucial to understanding the practical education that Isocrates espouses and criticizes others for not providing.

Education, then, must promote the practice of internal rhetoric so that students will act in accordance with *kairos* and thereby gain and exhibit wisdom. This is Isocrates' charge to educators, but it sums up only part of the connection between rhetorical education—*logon paideia*—and internal rhetoric. Isocrates also argues that rhetorical education is itself internally persuasive. In the *Antidosis,* Isocrates claims that the desire to speak well helps people become "better and worthier" (§275), because to achieve honor the rhetor must support worthy causes. In studying what arguments and examples to use to persuade others, rhetors inevitably first persuade themselves:

> He will select from all the actions of men which bear upon his subject those examples which are the most illustrious and the most edifying; and, habituating himself to contemplate and appraise such examples, he will feel their influence not only in the preparation of a given discourse but in all the actions of his life. (§277)

Thus research, which we might call self-education, is a way of performing internal rhetoric, and this internal rhetoric must take place prior to public rhetoric. Rhetors must persuade themselves to a certain *ēthos* before they can persuade their audience with their *ēthoi.* To recognize that efforts to educate oneself for rhetorical action in the world also have an ethical/rhetorical effect on the rhetor is to recognize, implicitly, that language forms us as much as we form it. Rhetoric is an ethically formative activity, and education entails internal rhetoric.

This examination of Isocrates, then, answers some questions left open at the close of the section on the *Iliad.* While the descriptions of internal rhetoric in the *Iliad* suggest a relationship or correspondence between internal rhetoric and *aretē,* Isocrates is very specific in describing internal rhetoric as the characteristic practice of wise people. He does so by equating good reasoning ability with the ability to speak publicly—both falling under the rubric of *logos.* Further, Isocrates tells us that the wise person uses internal rhetoric to grasp *kairos,* a sense of appropriateness or timeliness that makes action ethical and wise. This kairotic deliberation is evidenced in the *Iliad,* where the heroes must sometimes decide among competing cultural imperatives to determine what action at that particular moment would maintain their *aretē.* Isocrates goes beyond just using internal rhetoric to apply previously internalized cultural imperatives, however. In describing the education of the rhetor, he argues that people can consciously control the internalized models that become the premises for future kairotic decisions and actions.

Another question left open in the discussion of the *Iliad* was the applicability of internal rhetoric to different social classes. While it would be grossly misleading to claim that Isocrates educates or writes about anyone but elite boys and men, he does enumerate the private as well as the public benefits of *logos.* Just as everyone uses *logos* to make judgments about occurrences and people in their lives, everyone can use internal rhetoric to achieve *kairos* in their speech and actions. This tension between the inclusive possibilities of internal rhetoric and the exclusive concerns of the philosophers and rhetoricians I use to discuss internal rhetoric continues until the twentieth century, when rhetorical theory itself becomes more inclusive of speech genres available to a broader range of people.

Together, the *Iliad* and Isocrates provide a robust literary and philosophical beginning for historicizing a concept of internal rhetoric. In each, internal rhetoric is used not only for kairotic decision making but also to clarify situations or thoughts—it has, in other words, an epistemic as well as an ethical function, both in the service of reasoned action. However, internal rhetoric does not subsequently maintain this epistemic function, in part due to Plato's separation of thought/philosophy from speech/rhetoric. Although Plato sees the soul as multipartite, as it appears in the *Iliad,* and sees thought as internal conversation, as does Isocrates, his views on the hegemonic power of reason make Plato fit only ambiguously into a history of internal rhetoric. Aristotle completes the process of marginalizing internal rhetoric with a compartmentalization of linguistic *technai* even more thorough than Plato's. The next two sections, then, outline a philosophical movement that limits the concept of internal rhetoric and, in effect, forces it underground as long as the mainstream of rhetorical theory defines itself as an "other" in relation to post-Socratic philosophy.

Plato: Analysis and Inner Actions of the Psychē

Trying to determine what Plato might say about a concept like internal rhetoric, which transgresses the boundaries of the usual categories of linguistic *technai* attributed to him, is even more difficult than trying to determine what Plato says about rhetoric.[36] In this section I make two paradoxical claims about Plato and internal rhetoric. First, the biggest apparent hurdle to internal rhetoric in Plato—his disciplinary fragmentation of *logos* and his subsequent attribution of wisdom and thought to dialectic rather than to rhetoric—is not as much of a hurdle as it seems. Second, I argue that the most promising aspect of Platonic thought for internal rhetoric—his depiction of the soul as multipartite and internally interactive—is actually that aspect which limits the possibilities for internal rhetoric, both for him and for subsequent philosophers.

As I noted earlier in this chapter, Plato was the first philosopher to abandon the sophists' unified concept of *logos* and to coin words (and disciplines) like *eristikē, dialektikē, antilogikē,* and *rhētorikē* for distinct types of linguistic arts (see Schiappa 6, 44). Certainly, the Platonic ideal is to keep concepts separate; in the *Phaedrus,* Socrates describes the dialectic technique underpinning all good rhetoric:[37] "First, you must know the truth concerning everything you are speaking or writing about; you must learn how to define each thing in itself; and, having defined it, you must know how to divide it into kinds until you reach something indivisible" (*Phaedrus* 277b). Further, in the *Ion* Socrates argues that each *technē* has its own exclusive body of subject matter, with no overlap between disciplines (537d–38a).

In practice, however, Plato (usually through his character, Socrates) does not use these disciplinary terms in as consistent a manner as he might. It is characteristic of the dialogues, especially the early ones, that the attempt to define a key term (like *aretē* in the *Protagoras*) ends in perplexity, *aporia.* In the *Sophist,* for example, the Eleatic Stranger demonstrates particular virtuosity at coming up with multiple definitions through divisions and collections. Sophistry is defined initially as "appropriation, taking possession, hunting, animal-hunting, hunting on land, human hunting, hunting by persuasion, hunting privately, and money-earning" (223b). It is also "the expertise of the part of acquisition, exchange, selling, wholesaling, and soul-wholesaling, dealing in words and learning that have to do with virtue—that's sophistry in its second appearance" (224c–d) and "the money-making branch of expertise in debating, disputation, controversy, fighting, combat, and acquisition" (226a). Platonic dialogues frequently offer alternative definitions that are never resolved into a final, accepted definition.

Thus, we cannot assume that because Plato coined a variety of specific words for linguistic arts, he maintained consistent distinctions between those arts. True, in the *Gorgias* Socrates offers Polus a seemingly precise set of comparisons on sophistic and rhetoric: "What cosmetics is to gymnastics, sophistry is to legislation, and what pastry baking is to medicine, oratory *[rhetorikē]* is to justice" (465c). That is, sophistry is a fraudulent way of treating issues having to do with future actions, and rhetoric is a fraudulent way of treating issues of past conduct. But immediately after that comparison, he recognizes that such distinctions do not always hold in practice: "However, as I was saying, although these activities are naturally distinct in this way, yet because they are so close, sophists and orators *[rhētores]* tend to be mixed together as people who work in the same area and concern themselves with the same things" (465c). In the *Gorgias,* then, Socrates posits a classification that he must immediately qualify, manifesting a precision and indecision similar to that which the Eleatic Stranger shows in his definitions in the *Sophist.*

In the *Phaedrus,* Plato is still concerned with defining rhetoric, and again he offers a variety of definitions that do not necessarily resolve into one. Most important for my discussion is the broad definition that Socrates offers to Phaedrus:

> Isn't the rhetorical art *[rhētorikē],* taken as a whole, a way of directing the soul by means of speech, not only in the lawcourts and on other public occasions but also in private *[idiois]*? Isn't it one and the same art whether its subject is great or small, and no more to be held in esteem—if it is followed correctly—when its questions are serious than when they are trivial? (261a–b)

Phaedrus counters this broad definition with one we consider more traditional—"artful speaking and writing . . . mainly in the lawcourts; also perhaps in the Assembly" (261b)—but Socrates replies that this narrower viewpoint is held only by certain writers, and he reasserts his broader definition: "We can therefore find the practice of speaking on opposite sides *[antilogikē]* not only in the lawcourts and in the Assembly. Rather, it seems that one single art—if, of course, it is an art in the first place—governs all speaking" (261d–e). The broad definition of rhetoric that Socrates defends in this passage militates against the preconception that Plato uses *rhetorikē* only to refer to public oratory. Clearly, Plato sees the *technē* of language as applicable in both public and private discourse situations, just as Isocrates does—leaving open the possibility that Plato might acknowledge a rhetoric that occurs within the *psychē* as well as among people.[38]

Moreover, it is not clear that the different terms that Plato uses for language arts really refer to distinct *technai*. Socrates and Phaedrus use a variety of terms in discussing what they appear to agree is the same area of expertise: "When is a speech well written and delivered, and when is it not" (*logon opē kalōs echei legein te kai graphein,* 259e), "the art of speaking" (*logōn technē,* 260d), "the rhetorical art" (*rhētorikē,* 261a), "artful speaking and writing" (*legetai te kai graphetai technē,* 261b), and "the practice of speaking on opposite sides" (*antilogikē,* 261d). The apparent synonymy of these usages argues against attempting to distinguish rigidly between the Platonic *-ikē* neologisms for language arts.

Even the central Platonic dichotomy between rhetoric and dialectic, with which he distinguishes his teaching from that of the other sophists, gets fuzzy in places. One distinction Plato makes between the two *technai* is that the goal of dialectic is truth, while the goal of rhetoric is belief or persuasion *rather than* truth or knowledge.[39] But these different goals are not allowed to stand unchallenged; Plato has Socrates attribute to a personified Rhetoric *(logon technē)* the argument that "I am not forcing anyone to learn how to make speeches without knowing the truth; on the contrary, my advice, for what it is worth, is to take me up only after mastering the truth" (*Phaedrus* 260d). Subsequently, Socrates sketches the requirements for a true art of rhetoric, based on knowledge about kinds of souls and the types of speech needed to lead them to the truth (271d–72b)—a rhetoric that is virtually indistinguishable from dialectic, as many scholars have pointed out.[40] The *Phaedrus* thus portrays a rhetoric that approaches dialectic in its goals and relation to its audience.

Undermining the dichotomy from the dialectic side is the highly rhetorical nature of the Platonic dialogues, which many commentators argue are meant to enact philosophical dialectic (Cicero 18).[41] Rather than being disinterested conversations in which each participant (including Socrates) is equally as pleased to be refuted as to refute (*Gorgias* 458a), the dialogues often show Socrates to be as obstinate and manipulative in maintaining his position as any of his interlocutors.[42] Moreover, dialogues like the *Apology,* the *Menexenus,* the *Symposium,* and the *Phaedrus* either are orations themselves or they center on orations. Like Plato's attempt to distinguish between sophistry and rhetoric in the *Gorgias,* his distinction between rhetoric and dialectic works better in theory than in practice.

The ambiguities between rhetoric and dialectic are particularly evident when these categories are applied to mental phenomena. In the *Theaetetus,* for example, Socrates describes thought as an internal conversation: "a talk which the soul has with itself about the objects under its consideration" (189e; see also *Sophist* 263e–64b). This much of Socrates' analysis sounds a lot like what I have pointed out as occurring in the *Iliad* and being described by Isocrates. He elaborates on this description, though, in a way that moves it closer to dialectic:

> It seems to me that the soul when it thinks is simply carrying on a discussion *[dialogos]* in which it asks itself questions and answers them itself, affirms and denies. And when it arrives at something definite, either by a gradual process or a sudden leap, when it affirms one thing consistently and without divided counsel, we call this its judgment. (189e–90a)

Plato gives the question-and-answer format of dialectic great importance in the dialogues (see, e.g., *Cratylus* 390c, *Protagoras* 336c, *Gorgias* 454c), and his description of the dialectical search for the "quintessence" in *Letter VII* is strikingly similar to the above passage:

> Only when all these things—names, definitions, and visual and other perceptions—have been rubbed against one another and tested, pupil and teacher asking and answering questions in good will and without envy—only then, when reason and knowledge are at the very extremity of human effort, can they illuminate the nature of any object. (344b)

Thus, Plato might argue that the internal conversation is more dialectical than rhetorical—if that is a difference we are willing to grant him. Given the questions raised above about distinguishing between rhetoric and dialectic, a Platonic version of internal rhetoric can hardly be ruled out with the objection that his descriptions of thought as internal conversation partake of dialectic.[43] Taken together, then, Plato's characterizations of thought and the language arts leave room for a Platonic conception of internal rhetoric.

On the other hand, Plato's description of the makeup of the *psychē* provides much more ambiguous support for internal rhetoric than might be imagined. The writings previously discussed in this chapter have not explicitly located internal rhetoric in the *psychē,* but between the *thumos* and the *phrēn* (Homer) and in some undifferentiated mental space (Isocrates).[44] Plato's discussions of the *psychē* embody a new, probably Socratic emphasis on the *psychē* in the development of Greek thought, that it is the essence or true self of human beings, the seat of intelligence and consciousness (T. M. Robinson 3). Thus, if internal rhetoric were to take place within the *psychē* for Plato, it would assume a central role in activities that define humans *qua* humanity.

In Plato's early works, such as the *Phaedo,* the *psychē* is seen to be unitary: "The soul is most like the divine, deathless, intelligible, uniform, indissoluble, always the same as itself" (80b). Intrapersonal conflicts are between the *psychē* and the body *(soma)* rather than within the *psychē,* although the *psychē* can be "tainted" by being too closely concerned with bodily desires and concerns (81b). This intellectualized, unitary conception of the *psychē* is generally considered to be Socratic, and it gives way to the Platonic multipartite self most explicitly in the *Republic.*[45]

Book 4 of the *Republic* posits that the individual *psychē* has three parts, corresponding to the three classes in the republic—the guardians, the military, and the tradesmen—and the three virtues—wisdom, courage, and temperance (*sōphrosynē,* 435b)—the balance among which, in each case, constitutes justice. The three parts of the soul are the rational *(logistikos)*, the high-spirited *(thumikos)*, and the appetitive *(epithumētikos,* 439d–e). In the just *psychē,* the spirit or *thumos* aligns itself with reason to constrain the desires (440a–c).[46] Plato thus outlines a *psychē* with multiple, interacting parts, a scene that initially looks conducive to internal rhetoric.[47]

The glimpses Plato gives of the interaction of these parts is a long way from the rhetorical-dialectical mental conversation depicted in the *Theaetetus* and the *Sophist,* however. Instead, when the parts of the *psychē* are shown in "personified interchange," the interaction is characterized by coercion. In the *Republic,* immediately after delineating the parts of the soul, Socrates gives the following metaphor for the *thumos:*

> What happens if . . . he believes that someone has been unjust to him. Isn't the spirit *[thumos]* within him boiling and angry, fighting for what he believes to be just? Won't it endure hunger, cold, and the like and keep on till it is victorious, not ceasing from noble actions until it either wins, dies, or calms down, *called to heel by the reason [logos] within him, like a dog by a shepherd*? (440c–d, emphasis added)

Instead of psychic components interacting dialogically "in good will and without envy" (*Letter VII* 344b), the picture is one of a hierarchical, command-driven interaction.

An even more violent picture of this psychic coercion is drawn in Socrates' second speech in the *Phaedrus,* where the parts of the soul are compared to a chariot driver and his two horses. Socrates divides the *psychē* into three parts with distinct functions and associations: the charioteer, in control and attempting to guide the *psychē* toward "reality" or the realm of ideas; the white horse, amenable to control, enabling the charioteer to reach his goals, and associated with honesty, temperance, and modesty; and the dark horse, recalcitrant, lustful, and irascible.[48] This multipartite soul would seem to be an ideal location for internal rhetoric, but for Plato, the interaction between the three parts is again more coercive than dialogical. True, the dark horse does use language to try to influence its colleagues (along with trying to drag them along willy-nilly):

> [The dark horse], once it has recovered from the pain caused by the bit and its fall, bursts into a torrent of insults as soon as it has caught its breath, accusing its charioteer and yokemate of all sorts of cowardice and unmanliness for abandoning their position and their agreement *[homologia].* Now once more it tries to make its unwilling partners advance, and gives in grudgingly only when they beg it to wait until later. Then, when the promised time arrives, and they are pretending to have forgotten, it reminds them. (254c–d)

The dark horse's use of language to influence the behavior of its companions anticipates Socrates' subsequent description of the "rhetorician who does not know good from bad" (*rhētorikos agnoōn agathon kai kakon,* 260c). Not only does the dark horse have improper aims and motivations, but it is the wrong member to lead the team by its very nature—it is the appetites, misshapen and ugly. Socrates does not admit the possibility of any situation in which the dark horse of the appetites might validly move the soul by rhetorical or any other means.[49]

The proper part of the soul to influence the behavior of the whole is the charioteer. He rules not by rhetoric but by physical control and coercion:

> The charioteer is now struck with the same feelings as before, only worse, and he's falling back as he would from a starting gate; and he violently yanks the bit back out of the teeth of the insolent horse, only harder this time, so he bloodies its foul-speaking *[kakēloria]* tongue and jaws, sets its legs and haunches firmly on the ground, and gives it over to pain. (254e)

Modern readers might find this a bit grisly, but for Socrates, the charioteer is obviously the moral center of the metaphor. The charioteer has the foresight (*pronoia,* 254e) to strive toward the truth because of his position in the strict hierarchy of the *psychē*—since the charioteer properly guides the soul, he has the "correct" goals, just as the dark horse is improperly motivated by its very definition.

If the charioteer represents the controlling part of the *psychē,* then, the *psychē* is not dependent on language—at least in the *Phaedrus*—for self-direction. What little internal rhetoric seen so far, on the part of the dark horse, is far from privileged; it is both ineffective and directed toward base ends. Plato's teleology of souls in the *Phaedrus* even moves away from internal rhetoric, for the chariots of the gods' souls have two white horses and thus a natural tropism toward the good. Inverting the movement from the visual to the linguistic nature of thought noted in Isocrates, Plato privileges the visual nature of thought in the *Phaedrus* and posits *eros* as the source of both contention and coordinated movement among all three parts of the soul (see Guthrie 6:478).

In the *Republic* and the *Phaedrus,* Plato has provided us with a clear picture of an articulated soul that could provide a locus of internal rhetoric, but does not yet in the passages examined. Instead, the tripartite soul is a scene of coercion and hierarchical force, and internal rhetoric is not the source of *aretē* but (in the *Phaedrus*) a sign of manipulation by the dark horse of passion. I would like to examine one more passage in the *Republic,* however, that suggests the possibility of internal rhetoric in the Platonic partitioned soul:

> I suppose that someone who is healthy and moderate with himself goes to sleep only after having done the following: First, he rouses *[egeirō]* his rational part and feasts it on fine arguments and speculations; second, he neither starves nor feasts his appetites, so that they will slumber and not disturb his best part with either their pleasure or their pain, but they'll leave it alone, pure and by itself, to get on with its investigations, to yearn after and perceive something, it knows not what, whether it is past, present, or future; third, he soothes his spirited part in the same way, for example, by not falling asleep with his spirit still aroused after an outburst of anger. And when he has quieted these two parts and aroused the third, in which reason resides, and so takes his rest, you know that it is then that he best grasps the truth and that the visions that appear in his dreams are least lawless. (571d-572b)

This passage differs from the chariot metaphor in the *Phaedrus* in that there appears to be an unnamed fourth part of the *psychē*—the "he" that is the agent acting on the other three parts of the soul—that can rhetorically influence the rational part. In other words, there must be a part of the soul outside of the strict hierarchy set up earlier in the *Republic* that enjoys an egalitarian relationship with the rational part of the soul, allowing it to legitimately influence the latter. Even the other parts of the *psychē,* which have previously been portrayed as bestial, are accommodated rather than coerced, so the possibility of rhetorical interaction between the parts of the *psychē* appears less bleak here than in the other passages.

Again, as I noted in Isocrates, there is an unspecified space for mental dialogue that allows internal rhetoric to take place. The use of "fine arguments and speculations" *(logōn kalōn kai skepseōn)* to arouse and entertain might be similar to Isocrates' claims for the rhetorical efficacy of reading illustrious works. Moreover, in this final passage, internal rhetoric is at least coexistent with *aretē,* instead of antithetical to it as in the *Phaedrus.*

Plato thus leaves my historical reconstruction of internal rhetoric with a fertile mixture of tantalizing possibilities and constricting hierarchies. Plato's broad definition of rhetoric in the *Phaedrus* and description of thought as conversation in the *Theaetetus* both imply a holistic view of *logos* that could accommodate internal rhetoric.

Further, Plato offers an analysis of the *psychē* that, like the Homeric articulated mind, may or may not provide a place for dialogue. What limits a Platonic conception of internal rhetoric, though, is that he characterizes intrapsychic interactions as hierarchical because he elevates the rational part of the soul to a divine status. Internal rhetoric, as mental negotiation, cannot be considered an ethically legitimate practice if a unified, hegemonic rationality is always in control of a "healthy" soul. With this classical portrait of internal rhetoric delimited so far, I now turn to that most prominent of rhetorical codifiers in classical Greece, Aristotle, to argue that his divorce of private deliberation from rhetoric operates to the detriment of both concepts.

Aristotle: Internal Rhetoric Willy-Nilly

No sketch of this period would be complete without at least a glance at Aristotle. Yet Aristotle is my most hostile witness to date for a contribution to a theory of internal rhetoric. First, Aristotle has traditionally been thought of as the codifier of public, civic rhetoric.[50] The *Rhetoric* is our earliest extant source for the division of rhetoric into three public genres, defined by the possible roles of an external audience (1358a 36–1358b 8). William Grimaldi emphasizes the "important role which A[ristotle] gives to the auditor in his theory: rhetoric is concerned primarily with discourse (spoken or written) which is directed to another" (1:56). Aristotle is thus the primary source for the feeling expressed in the preface that "internal rhetoric" is an oxymoron.

Second, Aristotle is the grand systematizer or classifier, encouraging us to look at his discrete sciences or *technai* rather than at the spaces in between and connecting them. Internal rhetoric, however, seems to fit in the interstices of human life—between action and reflection, wisdom and speech, reason and the appetites. Instead of taking Aristotle on his own terms and saying that his philosophy does not allow for the possibility of an internal rhetoric, I want to probe his writings to see how internal rhetoric fits into Aristotelean discussions of rhetoric and ethics. I focus, therefore, on two places in the *Nichomachean Ethics* where a concept of internal rhetoric would help Aristotle out a little: in his discussion of deliberation and in his subsequent explanation of *phronēsis*.

Deliberation is the closest Aristotle comes to a concept of internal rhetoric, and his treatment of it in the *Ethics* has many correlations with his discussion of deliberative rhetoric in the *Rhetoric*.[51] In both books, he notes that we deliberate about things with variable outcomes that may be affected by or effected through our actions (*Ethics* 3.3.7–10; *Rhetoric* 1359a 32–38). Another commonality between the books is that Aristotle describes deliberation in terms of syllogistic reasoning, just as he calls enthymemes (rhetorical syllogisms) "the 'body' *[sōma]* of persuasion" in the *Rhetoric* (1354a 3). In his discussion of "deliberative excellence" *(euboulia)*, for example, Aristotle writes, "It is possible to arrive at a good conclusion, as well as at a bad one, by a false process of reasoning *[pseudēs syllogismos]*; one may arrive at what is the right thing to do, but not arrive at it on the right grounds, but by means of a wrong middle term" (*Ethics* 6.9.5). The conclusion of the syllogism is the action to be performed or the end to be reached; the premises have to do with what general principles should be followed (determined by the moral virtues) and what the particular facts of the situation at hand are (*Ethics* 6.7.7, 6.12.6, 6.12.10, 6.13.7). So far, this sounds very much like the types of internal rhetoric I found in both the *Iliad*, where the heroes apply cultural precepts to their immediate situations, and Isocrates, who says that wise people use a similar process to determine the *kairos* of a situation. Why, then, does Aristotle fail to acknowledge the rhetorical nature of personal deliberation?

The key disconnection between internal rhetoric and deliberation is Aristotle's failure to associate deliberation with an interaction among the various faculties *[dynameis]* of the *psychē*. Like Plato, he sees the *psychē* as divided, but in more complex ways than Plato's tripartite division. In the *Nichomachean Ethics*, he starts with a basic distinction between the rational and irrational *(logos* and *alogos)* parts of the *psychē* (1.13.9–10), dividing the former into the scientific *(epistēmonikos)* and calculative *(logistikos)* faculties (6.1.5–6) and the latter into the vegetative and appetitive faculties (1.13.18).[52] He does not see these faculties interacting in the same kind of "personified interchange" that was depicted in the *Iliad*, however. Rather, each faculty tends to have its own discrete sphere of functionality: The scientific faculty has to do with invariable objects and the calculative with variable, "since, on the assumption that knowledge is based on a likeness or affinity of some sort between subject and object, the parts of the soul adapted to the cognition of objects that are of different kinds must themselves differ in kind" (*Nichomachean Ethics*

6.1.5). Although the faculties do form various combinations—wisdom *(sophia)*, for example, is a "combination of Intelligence *[noos]* and Scientific Knowledge *[epistēmē]*" (6.7.3)—and dependencies—prudence *(phronēsis)* requires both cleverness *(deinotēs)* and intellectual virtue *(dianoētikos aretē)* (6.12.9–10), they are not portrayed as interacting dialogically in the process of deliberation.

Deliberation does involve more than one faculty, but Aristotle's strict division of functionality among the faculties means that it involves them in structurally discrete ways. Although Aristotle argues that the person, "as an originator of action, is a union of desire and intellect" (6.2.5), desire and intellect play separate roles in correct deliberation. Moral virtue *(ēthikos aretē)*, that of the appetitive soul, determines what ends we pursue, while practical wisdom *(phronēsis)* determines the means used (6.12.6, 6.13.7). In fact, according to Aristotle, *phronēsis* is what "regulates" moral virtues (6.13)—what makes desires virtuous—so there is little room for desire or appetite as an independently participating interlocutor in Aristotelean deliberation.

Even when Aristotle portrays the faculties as interacting, he does so in the same kind of hierarchical, nonrhetorical way that Plato does in book 4 of the *Republic*. In *De Anima,* Aristotle notes, "Sometimes [the appetite] overcomes the will *[boulēsis]* and sways it, as one sphere moves another; or appetite influences appetite, when the subject lacks self-control (but in nature the upper sphere always controls and moves the lower)" (434a 13–16). Like Plato, Aristotle believes that reason—"the upper sphere"—"naturally" controls the other faculties and thus no legitimate internal dialogue can take place. For both Plato and Aristotle, "in nature" *(physikos)* does not mean "normally" or "what most people do." Rather, it reflects a teleological—and hence, ethical—perspective: the ideal state, the "end" of humankind.

It is no surprise, then, that Aristotle compares deliberation to solving a geometry problem: "For when deliberating one seems in the procedure described to be pursuing an investigation or analysis that resembles the analysis of a figure in geometry" (3.3.11). In contrast to his holistic approach to rhetoric, encompassing irrational as well as rational appeals, Aristotle has thus limited deliberation to an intellectual exercise.

The problem with this conception of deliberation is that it does not account for the emotive or appetitive component of choice. Aristotle's description of deliberation is given to explain the phenomenon of choice, which he subsequently defines as "thought related to desire or desire related to thought" (6.2.5). But deliberation as he analyzes it only explains the reasoning part of the definition; it does not explain how the appetites are aligned with the result of deliberation, or what the motivation is to take the first step (determined by deliberation) toward the desired end. Lacking an explanation of how deliberation guides the appetites, Aristotle misses the rhetorical nature of deliberation, a connection that he clearly prepares us for in other ways, as I have argued.

Aristotle's account of deliberation is thus insufficient to explain the nature of choice, because it fails to explain how the appetites are aligned with reason through deliberation or how the resulting "deliberative desire" initiates action toward the desired end. Maybe this is why he is not quite sure that he has figured out *phronēsis:* while he treats the more public forms of *phronēsis* in the *Politics,* the *Rhetoric,* and the *Oeconimicus,* of personal *phronēsis* he says only that "the proper conduct of one's own affairs is a difficult problem, and requires consideration" (*Ethics* 6.8.4).

This rather irreverent exercise in using the perspective of internal rhetoric to look at a body of theory that seems to obviate it has added a few considerations to the concept of internal rhetoric. In the first place, this exercise points out the importance of both reason (rationality, *logos)* and the emotions (desires, *pathos)* to the operation of internal rhetoric. Second, although I have previously argued that both persuasion and clarification that result in reasoned actions are part of internal rhetoric, looking at Aristotle encourages me to emphasize aspects of persuasion and motivation within the umbrella term. Whether he wants to or not, Aristotle adds to a theory of internal rhetoric its importance for choice and purposive human action.

I have, so far, constructed a model of how internal rhetoric might have looked in classical Greece, adding the first historical layer to the core definition of internal rhetoric posed in the preface. In doing so, I have delineated several attributes of internal rhetoric that will be manifested in various ways in later eras.

My first task was to establish that ancient Greeks did indeed perceive thought to take on the characteristics of a dialogue with internally persuasive characteristics. This becomes apparent as early as the *Iliad,* in which various heroes talk to themselves in order to clarify situations, reinforce convictions, or make decisions in the midst of battle. Isocrates, too, takes as an assumption the fact that people talk to themselves, and he uses that fact to justify the teaching of rhetoric.

Another characteristic of internal rhetoric during this time is a sense that it takes place among different faculties or entities within the individual. For Homer, this roughly translates into a conversation between different mental organs of the mind and the will, although the voices in their internal dialogues reflect various cultural and biological imperatives that cannot be easily resolved into what later cultures will abstract as the voice of Reason or of the Emotions. Isocrates fails to distinguish specific mental agents, but Plato and Aristotle make up for this lack by multiplying faculties within the *psychē*—even if they do not perceive them to be persuading each other. These different faculties (*dynameis,* functions now rather than the Homeric mental "organs") include the reason (practical and speculative), will, and emotions or appetites.

With the theory that parts of the *psychē* interact with one another comes a question about the nature of that interaction; and here I find varying accounts among my sources. For Homer and particularly for Isocrates, the internal interaction is one of persuasive dialogue and clarification for oneself. Isocrates also suggests that studying model texts is a way of persuading oneself to a better character. For Plato and Aristotle, for whom the parts of the *psychē* exist in a hierarchy of value and power, the ideal interaction is one of successful coercion of the "lower" parts of the soul by the "higher." Plato only hints at the possibility of legitimate persuasive interaction with the rational part of the soul, and Aristotle misses this capability by failing to connect deliberation, his closest equivalent to internal rhetoric, with the parts of the soul enumerated in *De Anima* or the *Nichomachean Ethics* and with the affective realm so important to his rhetoric. By his very omission, Aristotle makes it apparent that the emotions or affective part of the soul is an important aspect of internal rhetoric, and therefore that internal rhetoric is not just a catachresis for "logic" or "reasoning."

Since I form my central description of classical internal rhetoric on the Isocratean model of persuasive dialogue, it is useful to compare that formulation to my discussions of the *Iliad,* Plato, and Aristotle. I argue that Isocrates' treatment of *logos* provides an internal rhetoric that allows people to grasp the *kairos* of the situation they are in: to speak, act, or decide appropriately to the time and situation, but still in a principled manner. This description of how internal rhetoric functions is borne out by further examination of the *Iliad,* in which the heroes use internal rhetoric to decide the appropriate action for them to take in battle, and of Aristotle, who characterizes prudence *(phronēsis)* as the ability to make decisions according to moral virtue and the situation at hand. Attention to *kairos* is less evident in Plato, who characterizes dialogic thought as a search for (eternal) truths in the *Theaetetus* and *Phaedrus,* but may be implied in the description of the virtuous person's nocturnal state of mind in *Republic* 9.

Of course, the Isocratean model assumes that internal rhetoric is an ethical activity, and that is not a universal assumption during the classical period. Homer definitely associates internal rhetoric with a warrior's *aretē,* although the nature of the relationship—causal or coincidental—remains vague. Plato seems to go both ways on this issue, associating internal rhetoric with insolence in the chariot metaphor of the *Phaedrus,* but also associating it with the temperate person's nighttime ritual in the *Republic.* Aristotle does not recognize the existence of internal rhetoric, but he values its close relative, deliberation, very highly as the definitive activity of *phronēsis* or practical wisdom. What Plato and Aristotle do add to this consideration of the ethics of internal rhetoric is the ideal of the *psychē* being controlled by reason and therefore the suspicion that unreasonable (and from an Isocratean standpoint, uncultivated) internal rhetoric is necessarily pernicious.

Finally, considering the demographic breadth of application that a concept of internal rhetoric might have, I again go back to an Isocratean point of view. In the *Iliad* it is not clear whether internal rhetoric aids the *aretē* of any social class other than the warrior class, since that is all that is portrayed. Isocrates, though, opens the possibility that internal rhetoric is a valuable mode of thought for all classes of society, since he argues that *logos* is central to the negotiation of both public and private matters. Both Plato and Aristotle hold to a hierarchical view of society and ethics parallel to their hierarchical view of the *psychē,* so it is probable that they would not view the capability of internal rhetoric as a widespread phenomenon—or, conversely, given their negative views on the insurgence of the appetites, they might consider it a practice of *hoi polloi* rather than the philosophers they are primarily concerned with.

By thus examining various classical texts, I have opened up a range of possibilities for internal rhetoric that will continue to play a role in subsequent conceptions of internal rhetoric. The association of internal rhetoric with rhetoric is carried forward by rhetoricians like Cicero, whose *De Oratore* matter-of-factly lists the self as one of a range of possible audiences for the rhetor:

> Eloquence . . . is one and the same, into whatever tracts or regions of debate it may be carried . . . whether to a small or to a large assembly—whether to strangers, to friends, or *alone*—its language is derived through different channels, not from different sources; and, wherever it directs its course, it is attended with the same equipment and decoration. (198, emphasis added)

There is a definite echo of Isocrates' insistence on the unity of *logos* in this passage (as well as Socrates' broad definition of rhetoric in the *Phaedrus*), and *De Oratore* is central to an understanding of Ciceronian rhetorical theory. So the question is not whether internal rhetoric continues to be an undercurrent in rhetorical history but whether theorizing about it over rhetorical history, particularly those periods characterized by a confluence of interest in psychology, ethics, and rhetoric, provides a useful framework for explaining moral action in the world. The next period that I will examine is the time of the Enlightenment in England, when moral philosophy (a combination of psychology and ethics) and rhetoric again enjoy a heyday of interest and speculation.

2

Moral Philosophy and Internal Rhetoric from Bacon to Whately

> But take care little fond foolish Heart remember the pain—the keen torturs which recently sunk the[e] to the depths of malancholy / drive from thee thy too great susceptibility! Shut every avenue which lays open the tender mind to soft distress!—My heart felt the gentle tho well-timed caution & assured me by its peaceful steady Vibration its fidelity to its owner.
>
> —Martha "Patty" Rogers diary, 2 October 1785

Between fourth-century B.C.E. Athens and seventeenth-century England, the study of rhetoric was both continuous—Isocratean *logon paideia* being transmitted through Cicero and Quintilian into medieval and Renaissance humanistic education in the trivium (grammar, rhetoric, and dialectic)—and transforming, as it adapted to changing cultural and political circumstances. Some or all of these changes, such as the rising hegemony of the Christian Church with its reworking of secular learning, would impinge upon a full recounting of the history of internal rhetoric during this same period. The histories of public and internal rhetoric are not entirely parallel, however: The death of the Roman Republic and subsequent disappearance of representative government in Europe during the following centuries, to which is often attributed a decline in substantive rhetorical theories, would not necessarily have the same results for a concurrent history of internal rhetoric. Instead—were this book a comprehensive history—I would be tracing the influences of the Stoics' intellectualism and practices of self-cultivation, the confessions of St. Augustine and the spiritual exercises of St. Ignatius Loyola, and the scholastic dominance of logic—known as *the* art of thinking—over rhetoric. Much remains to be discovered for a history of internal rhetorics to be told as thoroughly as that of public rhetorics. My present purpose being to demonstrate how rhetoric has been seen to be directed inwardly at various points in the past, I am selecting only a few historical texts to sketch the contours of a tradition as rich and multiform as that of public rhetorics.

This chapter is limited to discussions of internal rhetoric based on British philosophers who examine how the mental faculties interact—a school of thought I will label "faculty psychology." Although the term is usually used with reference to Thomas Reid's theory of innate mental faculties, I use it to differentiate moral philosophies that provide a highly rhetorical description of the interaction of the faculties from those that concentrate on the association of mental faculties with different sense perceptions. The concentration on faculty psychology in this chapter should not be understood to suggest that it is the only way to conceptualize internal rhetoric during this period: Hugh Blair, for example, follows Isocrates' and Quintilian's lead in seeing rhetorical education as internal rhetoric but does not use faculty psychology to explain the process.[1] On the other hand, many Renaissance and Enlightenment philosophers who discuss the faculties, like Thomas Hobbes and John Locke, avoid taking a rhetorical approach to mental processes. Hobbes uses the term *Mentall Discourse* in the *Leviathan,* but he describes it as a mechanistic replaying of motions originally generated in the senses (20). Locke sees the faculties as different powers of the mind and specifically rejects a Baconian, rhetorical approach to the faculties:

> This way of Speaking of *Faculties,* has misled many into a confused Notion of so many distinct Agents in us, which had their several Provinces and Authorities, and did command, obey, and perform several Actions, as so many distinct Beings; which has been no small occasion of wrangling, obscurity, and uncertainty in Questions relating to them. (237)

To Locke, the faculties are merely mental powers held by the agential self. Both Locke and Hobbes see the faculties as responding to external stimuli rather than internal interactions. Thus, the concentration in this chapter on faculty psychology does not imply a necessary connection between internal rhetoric and faculty psychology; on the contrary, I suggest in closing that faculty psychology breaks down as a vocabulary for describing internal rhetoric. Regardless of its adequacy as a "terminological screen" for internal rhetoric, though, faculty psychology is a historical bridge between the various conceptions of a multipartite soul in the previous chapter and the Freudian and post-Freudian psychologies that play a major role in the following two chapters.

I will focus on three writers who use a faculty psychology framework as the basis for their versions of internal rhetoric. The first, both logically and chronologically, is Sir Francis Bacon, the first author to base a discussion of rhetoric on the mental faculties rather than on a categorical scheme based on the rhetorical situation (e.g., audience, occasion, issue; Cogan 213–14). After demonstrating that Bacon integrates faculty psychology and rhetoric, both internal and external, from a philosophical perspective,[2] I explore how this same conjunction is approached from an ethical perspective by Anthony Ashley Cooper, the third earl of Shaftesbury. Shaftesbury is more renowned as a moral and aesthetic philosopher than as a rhetorician, but his *Soliloquy; or, Advice to an Author* is an argument for internal rhetoric, and he follows Bacon in arguing that there can be no moral action without it. I then briefly sketch discussions of the gendering of faculties and explore why internal rhetoric becomes less salient in the psychological and rhetorical theories of other major eighteenth-century philosophers. I close by examining Richard Whately's use of internal rhetoric to justify pathetic appeals in public rhetoric.

Francis Bacon and the New Psychology

Francis Bacon may seem an unlikely figure to play a crucial role in a history of internal rhetoric, given the unimportance of rhetoric in his scheme of human knowledge. He splits the classical canons of rhetoric among his four intellectual arts of invention, judgment, memory, and tradition, and relegates the term *rhetoric* itself to only a third part of the art of tradition,[3] "the Illustration of Tradition" (*Advancement* 296)—namely, style.[4] Even though Bacon sees rhetoric as stylistic, he considers it a crucial factor in ethical deliberation. Moreover, Bacon's treatment of how rhetoric functions psychologically offers the most extended explanation yet of the workings of internal rhetoric, because he implies that internal rhetoric is either indistinguishable from or prior to public rhetoric. Bacon thus provides a strong opening for this chapter's examination of faculty psychology and internal rhetoric.

Bacon's explanation for the relationships among the mental faculties is fundamental to his often-cited "definition" of rhetoric: "The duty and office of Rhetoric is *to apply Reason to Imagination* for the better moving of the will" (*Advancement* 297). According to Bacon, the will—the source of all resolution and voluntary action[5]—is subject to the influence of three faculties: reason, imagination, and the affections. Any two of the three is sufficient to direct the will, but the imagination tends to side with the affections because the goods desired by the affections are immediate and therefore more alive to the imagination:

> For the affections themselves carry ever an appetite to good, as reason doth; the difference is, that *the affection beholdeth merely the present; reason beholdeth the future and sum of time;* and therefore the present filling the imagination more, reason is commonly vanquished. (*Advancement* 299)

So far, this description of faculty psychology is somewhat reminiscent of Plato's chariot analogy, with both reason and the affections (or, for Plato, the appetites) stimulated by the sight of an apparent good and struggling toward their desired objects. The crucial difference, of course, is that Plato does not show reason being "vanquished," but having the upper hand by coercion over the appetites.

Instead of the coercive, hierarchical model of the faculties portrayed by Plato, Bacon offers one of confederacy among the faculties:

> In regard of the continual mutinies and seditions of the affections . . . reason would become captive and servile, if Eloquence of Persuasions did not practise and win the Imagination from the Affection's part, and contract a confederacy between the Reason and Imagination against the Affections. (*Advancement* 299)

Because Bacon's model of the faculties is negotiative rather than coercive, he sees rhetoric among the faculties as both possible and necessary for assuring the "government of reason." Rhetoric, rather than force, is the means by which reason is able to guide the proclivities of the mind.

Bacon's discussion of the interaction of the faculties is thus significantly different from that of Plato and Aristotle. Both of the classical philosophers portray a conflict between (roughly) reason and the emotions or appetites, but both argue that reason or the intellect naturally controls the *psychē*. The implications for internal rhetoric in each are ambiguous, if not morally culpable: if the natural or healthy *psychē* is guided by reason, then rhetoric is only necessary to guide diseased souls (see, e.g., *Gorgias* 480b–481b).[6] Logic and dialectic, which exclude emotional considerations, then become the paradigms for mental activity, especially for ethical deliberation.

Bacon, consciously or not,[7] inverts Plato's and Aristotle's views of the soul by insisting that the affections are not "naturally" governed by reason but must be persuaded by rhetoric: "Again, if the affections in themselves were pliant and obedient to reason, it were true there should be no great use of persuasions and insinuations to the will, more than of naked proposition and proofs" (*Advancement* 299). But because of the "continual mutinies and seditions of the affections," reason needs rhetorical "illustration" to control the will. For Bacon, logic alone is incapable of moving the mind to resolution or to action: "For the method of the Stoics, who thought to thrust virtue upon men by concise and sharp maxims and conclusions, which have little sympathy with the imagination and will of man, has been justly ridiculed by Cicero" (*De Augmentis* 9:133). Bacon thus emphasizes the crucial difference between moving the will to the desired action and merely demonstrating that something is so—the difference between rhetoric and logic. Instead of using the nonlogical aspects of rhetoric to "warp" reason, Bacon claims that their proper use is to make reason effective: "The end of Rhetoric is to fill the imagination to second reason, not to oppress it" (*Advancement* 298).

The significance of Bacon's definition of rhetoric as the application of "*Reason to Imagination* for the better moving of the will" is that rhetoric alone brings about reasoned actions. Marc Cogan notes the essential paradox of Baconian rhetoric:

> While on the one hand reducing the significance of rhetoric by removing its traditional powers of invention, arrangement, and so forth and by limiting its function to the embellishment of reasoning, Bacon at the same time gives to this newly circumscribed art a vastly extended importance. . . . He makes it the central and indispensable art for all rational action. (O'Rourke et al. 38)

And not only is rhetoric necessary for reasoned action; it is necessary for ethics as well. Since Bacon follows the classical model of ethics as behavior in accordance with reason, rhetoric is also the source of ethical behavior because it is guided by reason even though it is directed toward the imagination.[8]

Rhetoric enables reason to direct the will by enlivening the imagination's representation of future goods (perceptible only by reason): "But after that force of eloquence and persuasion hath made things future and remote appear as present, then upon the revolt of the imagination reason prevaileth" (*Advancement* 299). Rhetoric imaginatively makes future goods such as virtuous behavior or long-term goals, normally desired only by reason, seem vivid and desirable so that reason and the imagination can jointly direct the will. So rhetoric strengthens the appeal of reason to the motive faculty, the will, by making future goods seem "present" or immediate.

It does so by the "ornamentation of speech"—style, which brings us to the other side of the paradox between Bacon's limitation of rhetoric to style and his substantial claims for the ethical importance of rhetoric. Bacon's stylistic rhetoric is, according to Cogan, "nothing less than a grammar of the affective possibilities of language" ("Rhetoric and Action" 228). To illustrate the persuasive power of stylistic devices, Bacon himself uses two metaphors, presence and penetration. He introduces the metaphor of presence with reference to Plato:

> For Plato said eloquently (though it has now grown into a commonplace) "that virtue, if she could be seen, would move great love and affection"; and it is the business of rhetoric to make pictures of virtue and goodness, so that they may be seen. For since they cannot be showed to the sense in corporeal shape, the next degree is to show them to the imagination in as lively representation as possible, by ornament of words.[9] (*De Augmentis* 9:132–33; see also *Advancement* 298)

Like Plato, then, Bacon sees the psyche as driven by desire evoked by visual images. Unlike Plato, however, Bacon argues that the ornamentation of language, or stylistic rhetoric, is necessary to create the visual images that allow reason to dominate over the will. For Bacon, linguistic ornamentation generates presence by vividly or concretely representing abstract concepts or distant goals.

Bacon underscores the rhetorical efficacy of stylistic ornamentation with a second metaphor, one of penetration:

> There are many forms which, though they mean the same, yet affect differently; as the difference is great in the piercing of that which is

> sharp and that which is flat, though the strength of the percussion be the same. Certainly there is no man who will not be more affected by hearing it said, "Your enemies will be glad of this" . . . than by hearing it said only, "This will be evil for you." Therefore these points and stings of speech are by no means to be neglected. (*De Augmentis* 9:135–36)

From the example given, Bacon sees stylistic ornamentation—the "points and stings of speech"—also as taking advantage of the emotive impact of words. The noun *enemies* provides a more penetrating, because more concretely affective, image than the abstract *evil.* By using metaphors such as presence and penetration to describe how stylistic ornamentation works, Bacon emphasizes that the goal of rhetoric is not primarily to relay information (which is instead the goal of method), but to affect auditors in such a way that their wills are swayed in accordance with reason.[10]

So far in this section I have been using the term *rhetoric* as Bacon does, without distinguishing internal from public rhetoric, but clearly Bacon is referring to both. By prefacing his remarks with a discussion of classical rhetoricians and rhetors, he places himself within the classical canon of rhetorical theory and public practice, saying that because rhetoric is "a science excellent, and excellently well laboured," he will only comment on incidentals that "attend the art, rather than on the rules or use of the art itself" (*Advancement* 296, 297). Yet Bacon wants to "stir the earth a little about the roots of this science" (*Advancement* 297), and in doing so he primarily describes what happens within the individual psyche. Because of his psychological bent, much of what Bacon says about rhetoric applies to both external and internal discourse.

As I have noted, Bacon's description of "the duty and office of Rhetoric" is psychological and ethical rather than political or social: "*to apply Reason to Imagination* for the better moving of the will" (*Advancement* 297). Bacon classifies rhetoric with logic and ethics under "Human Knowledge which concerns the Mind" (*Advancement* 254), and he continues his psychological perspective on these arts when he relates them to three ways in which reason can be misled in its governance of the will: "by Illaqueation or Sophism, which pertains to Logic; by Imagination or Impression, which pertains to Rhetoric; and by Passion or Affection, which pertains to Morality" (*Ad-*

vancement 297). Indeed, Bacon sometimes seems to include the possibility of public rhetoric only as an aside:

> And as in *negotiation with others* men are wrought by cunning, by importunity, and by vehemency; so in *this negotiation within ourselves* men are undermined by Inconsequences, solicited and importuned by Impressions or Observations, and transported by Passions. (*Advancement* 297, emphases added)

Bacon apparently sees rhetoric primarily as a "negotiation within ourselves" with the purpose of coordinating the faculties under the guidance of reason. Because of his extensive discussion of the psychological and ethical functioning of rhetoric, it is easy to see Bacon as the first theorist I have examined to discuss primarily internal rather than public rhetoric.

Later in the chapter, Bacon attends more to an external audience, echoing Aristotle in his claim that "Rhetoric handleth [Reason] as it is planted in popular opinions and manners" (*Advancement* 300). But even here, Bacon is more concerned with private discourse than public oratory:

> The proofs and persuasions of Rhetoric ought to differ according to the auditors . . . which application, in perfection of idea, ought to extend so far, that if a man should speak of the same thing to several persons, he should speak to them all respectively and several ways. (*Advancement* 300)

Bacon has here virtually arrived at the same picture of an ideal rhetoric that Plato posits in the *Phaedrus,* that rhetors should understand the nature of individual souls so they may address each auditor in the most appropriate and effective way. Bacon's emphasis on the "politic part of eloquence in private speech" (*Advancement* 300) over public oratory is not surprising, given his project to suggest and address those sciences that need further development as well as to give a synopsis of existing sciences. But what is important for my purposes is that Bacon considers "the roots of this science" to be internal rhetoric, which is the only way public oratory and private conversations can have any effect on their intended auditors.

Bacon, then, has provided a detailed explanation of internal rhetoric. In Bacon's version of faculty psychology, reason does not necessarily dominate the other faculties, because the will is drawn toward the good that is most present in the imagination. Typically, the affections determine this present good, because the objects they desire are immediate and concrete. Internal rhetoric shifts the balance of power among the faculties, making the goods desired by reason, which tend to be long-term or abstract, present to the imagination by attractively portraying them with the ornaments of speech.

In this analysis of the faculties, internal rhetoric becomes necessary to ensure the governance of reason over the will and thus to ensure ethical action. Bacon's positive depiction of the interaction of the faculties differs markedly from the hierarchical models of Plato and Aristotle and so explains the difference between them in the valuation of internal rhetoric. At the same time, Bacon has stripped internal rhetoric of the epistemic function that Isocrates assigned it, limiting its scope to the (still very important) ethical management of the emotions and behavior. This characterization of internal rhetoric as ethical rather than epistemic will generally hold true for the authors discussed in the rest of this chapter, although Shaftesbury does argue that its ethical effect is based in the self-knowledge created by internal rhetoric.

Finally, Bacon's desire to "stir the earth a little about the roots of this science" and to propose necessary extensions to each science he discusses leads him to privilege internal rhetoric over public oratory, which he considers to have been adequately covered by earlier rhetoricians. Internal rhetoric becomes the paradigmatic form of rhetoric, with private conversation and public oratory being extensions and complications of this primary psychological act.

Bacon's derivation of internal rhetoric from the structure of the psyche provides a strong model of internal rhetoric that is variously reflected in psychological, ethical, and rhetorical theories of the seventeenth, eighteenth, and nineteenth centuries. In fact, it will fall to later writers to develop the full ethical implications of Bacon's description of internal rhetoric, with its guidance on bringing the will under the control of reason. Bacon himself misses the connection between his internal rhetoric and the "'*Regiment* or *Culture of the Mind*,' which I also call the *Georgics of the Mind* . . . prescribing rules how to accommodate the will of man [to the good]" (*De Augmentis* 9:194).[11] This passage is from Bacon's section on ethics, where he calls the "Georgics of the Mind" one of his "Desiderata" of sciences that need to be developed. Anthony Ashley Cooper, the third earl of Shaftesbury, embraces internal rhetoric precisely as the means of regulating the mind that Bacon desires. Let us now turn to Shaftesbury for an ethical-aesthetic perspective of faculty psychology and internal rhetoric.

Shaftesbury's "Sovereign Remedy" of Soliloquy

Shaftesbury is credited with being the inspiration for Scottish moral sense philosophy (Sambrook 55–57), and presaged its close connection to rhetoric for such philosophers as Henry Home, Lord Kames, and Adam Smith. Shaftesbury's relevance to internal rhetoric lies in his highly rhetorical approach to the same ethical problem that Bacon addressed: the need for reason to be bolstered against the emotions so it can control behavior. Even though he was a student of John Locke, Shaftesbury depicts the psyche as very much a site of internal dissension, and prescribes the cultivation of reasonable internal rhetoric as the only way to overcome the pernicious rhetoric of the emotions that would otherwise rule.[12]

Shaftesbury combines moral philosophy with rhetorical self-discipline in his treatise *Soliloquy; or, Advice to an Author,* which I argue constitutes an oddly Platonic internal rhetoric. First, I place *Soliloquy* in the context of Shaftesbury's moral and aesthetic philosophies. The theory of internal rhetoric developed in this work both depends on and is crucial to an understanding of Shaftesbury's concepts of moral sense and taste. I next analyze Shaftesbury's theory of internal rhetoric: his description of the faculties and of the process, ethical necessity, and purposes of internal rhetoric. Finally, I argue that Shaftesbury's presentation of internal rhetoric, which differs so greatly from the writers I have discussed previously, suggests his purpose in writing about internal rhetoric. Shaftesbury's presentation is important because he is less concerned with providing an accurate—or even ideal—analysis of the psyche than with persuading his audience to follow a certain aesthetic and ethical model of discourse and behavior.

Shaftesbury has a peculiarly aesthetic view of moral philosophy. He unites the human capacities of taste and moral sense because he believes the entire universe is ruled by proportion and harmony: "The proportionate and regular state is the truly prosperous and natural in every subject" (*Miscellaneous Reflections on the Preceding Trea-*

tises [Misc.] in *Characteristics* 2:267).[13] As Garland Brooks notes, "It is apparent that Shaftesbury's conceptions of beauty and morality were essentially identical; the one is a perception of external harmony, balance, and proportion, the other of inward" (438). Shaftesbury thus calls a state of psychological health both beautiful and moral:

> Should not this (one would imagine) be still the same case and hold equally as to the mind? . . . Is there no natural tenour, tone, or order of the passions or affections? No beauty or deformity in this moral kind? . . . Will it not be found in this respect, above all, "that what is beautiful is harmonious and proportionable; what is harmonious and proportionable is true; and what is at once both beautiful and true is, of consequence, agreeable and good"? (*Misc.* 2:268–69)

Because the good is united to the beautiful in their qualities of harmony and proportion, Shaftesbury's moral philosophy is highly aesthetic, and his arguments concerning taste and the moral sense often conjoin the two faculties.

Even though harmony and proportion are natural to the universe, human beings are born with no more than the capacity to develop an appreciation for them. Thus, people must apply themselves to proper study to develop both their moral sense and their taste:

> Now a taste or judgment, 'tis supposed, can hardly come ready formed with us into the world. Whatever principles or materials of this kind we may possibly bring with us, whatever good faculties, senses, or anticipating sensations and imaginations may be of Nature's growth, and arise properly of themselves, without our art, promotion, or assistance, the general idea which is formed of all this management and the clear notion we attain of what is preferable and principle in all these subjects of choice and estimation will not, as I imagine, by any person be taken for innate. Use, practice, and culture must precede the understanding and wit. (*Misc.* 2:257)

People are born, then, with differing propensities for recognizing the good and the beautiful and must develop their innate capabilities with practice. Shaftesbury thus attempts to bridge the "nature versus nurture" argument that has characterized rhetoric (among other arts) at least since Cicero.

Because people must develop their moral sense, the aesthetic nature of Shaftesbury's moral philosophy does not mean that it is divorced from pragmatic concerns. Rather, like Isocrates, Shaftesbury has a strict standard of practical benefit that he demands of his own and others' philosophies:

> As for metaphysics, and that which in the schools is taught for logic or for ethics, I shall willingly allow it to pass for philosophy when by any real effects it is proved capable to refine our spirits, improve our understandings, or mend our manners. (*Soliloquy* 188)

Shaftesbury thus separates himself largely from the empirical school of philosophy, which he considers to have a place in the body of human knowledge but not to have a claim on sciences having to do with human behavior.[14] Instead of this "super-speculative philosophy," Shaftesbury sees his own as "a more practical sort, which relates chiefly to our acquaintance, friendship, and good correspondence with ourselves" (*Soliloquy* 190). Perhaps the primary method that Shaftesbury offers for nurturing the moral sense is internal rhetoric, which he discusses in *Soliloquy.*

In this treatise, Shaftesbury presents a relationship among appetites, reason, and will similar to Bacon's, although with a slightly different analogy from Bacon's "confederacies":

> For Appetite, which is the elder brother to Reason, being the lad of stronger growth, is sure, on every contest, to take the advantage of drawing all to his own side. And Will, so highly boasted, is at best merely a top or football between these youngsters, who prove very unfortunately matched. (123)[15]

For Shaftesbury the appetites are naturally stronger than reason in controlling the will. But despite the image of brute strength raised by this metaphoric description, Shaftesbury soon makes it clear that the strength of the appetites is more in deceit than anything else:

> Those ["imaginations or fancies"] on the side of the elder brother Appetite are strangely subtle and insinuating. They have always the faculty to speak by nods and winks. By this practice they conceal half their meaning, and, like modern politicians, pass for deeply wise, and adorn themselves with the finest pretexts and most specious glosses imaginable. (123–24)

This, then, is a major difference between the psychologies of Bacon and Shaftesbury: Bacon does not attribute anything wicked to the affections, but only says that they desire present, rather than future or abstract, goods. Shaftesbury, like Plato, sees the appetites as actively bad because they are deceitful and work against the governance of reason.

Because both the strength and iniquity of the appetites lie in their deceptiveness, Shaftesbury describes his "remedy"—what I call internal rhetoric—as forcing the appetites to reveal themselves in their true natures:

> And here it is that our sovereign remedy and gymnastic method of soliloquy takes its rise: when by a certain powerful figure of inward rhetoric the mind apostrophises its own fancies, raises them in their proper shapes and personages, and addresses them familiarly, without the least ceremony or respect. By this means it will soon happen that two formed parties will erect themselves within. (123)

The two parties are those of the appetites and reason, and "the imaginations or fancies . . . are forced to declare themselves and take party" (123). But Shaftesbury does not portray the imagination as being the decisive factor in this conflict, as Bacon does. Instead, Shaftesbury sees the imagination as allied with the appetites—in fact, as the source of the appetites: "Thus I contend with fancy and opinion, and search the mint and foundery of imagination. For here the appetites and desires are fabricated; hence they derive their privilege and currency" (207). Even though Shaftesbury calls his practice "inward rhetoric," then, the model he follows in describing it is closer to Plato's agonistic model than to Bacon's inner negotiations.

Shaftesbury thus sees internal rhetoric as functioning in a very different manner from Bacon's description, even though both philosophers begin with the same components of the appetites, imagination, reason, and will. Their respective discussions of the ethical efficacy of internal rhetoric also have only partial similarity. For Bacon, people have a natural tropism for satisfying the appetites that is only interrupted by the practice of internal rhetoric. Internal rhetoric is thus an art that will be conducted in accordance with reason and so with ethical ends (although it may be perverted to propagate false impressions, *Advancement* 297). Shaftesbury, on the other hand, portrays two antagonistic parties in the psyche, either of which may practice rhetoric in its attempt to control the will. His "sovereign method of soliloquy" is, obviously, a prescription for how to make reason and its allies the effective orators, which he opposes to the uncultivated, iniquitous rhetoric of the appetites.[16]

The internal rhetoric that Shaftesbury wants people to cultivate is one that allows reason to gain control over the psyche. If it is practiced correctly, the appetites will be vanquished by reason as soon as they are revealed for what they are: "Being confronted with their fellows of a plainer language and expression, they are forced to quit their mysterious manner, and discover themselves mere sophisters and impostors who have not the least to do with the party of reason and good taste" (124). With regard to this cultivated internal rhetoric, the role of the appetites appears obstructionist rather than rhetorical in their own right:

> So that we may readily from hence conclude that the chief interest of ambition, avarice, corruption, and every sly insinuating vice is to prevent this interview and familiarity of discourse which is consequent upon close retirement and inward recess. 'Tis the grand artifice of villainy and lewdness, as well as of superstition and bigotry, to put us upon terms of greater distance and formality with ourselves, and evade our proving method of soliloquy. (115)

These vices, caused by submission to the appetites, can thus be avoided by the diligent practice of internal rhetoric, which allows a person to act and resolve in accordance with reason and therefore with morality. According to Shaftesbury, then, once this corrupt acquiescence to the appetites is cleared away, people prefer the reasonable and moral because we have a "natural moral sense" that leads them to prefer what is right unless this sense has been corrupted (*An Inquiry Concerning Virtue or Merit* in *Characteristics* 1:262).

If this reasonable kind of internal rhetoric is not cultivated, Shaftesbury argues that the passions will use their own brand of uncultivated rhetoric upon the will. This nonrational internal persuasion can have a subversive effect on ethical behavior:

> Can there be strength of mind, can there be command over oneself, if the ideas of pleasure, the suggestions of fancy, and the strong pleadings of appetite and desire are not often withstood, and the imaginations soundly reprimanded and brought under subjection? (202)

This darker side of internal rhetoric is closer to Plato's association of internal persuasion with the illicit desires of the dark horse than to Bacon's more innocuous description of the affections being drawn to present goods. Internal rhetoric directed by reason is thus all the more crucial in overcoming the immoral persuasions of the appetites.

Shaftesbury is also more specific than Bacon in delineating the benefits to be derived from internal rhetoric. Although his ostensible intent is to provide "Advice to Authors," he admits that this work has a much broader implicit purpose: "His pretense has been to advise authors and polish styles, but his aim has been to correct manners and regula[te] lives" (*Misc.* 2:272). Shaftesbury thus enumerates the practical benefits of his "sovereign remedy" both for personal lives, applicable to everyone, and for the professional concerns of authors. The most important are the personal benefits that the practice of cultivated internal rhetoric contributes: developing the moral sense and taste so that a person is governed by reason. Ancillary to personal development are various aspects of professional development for authors such as preventing the "froth and scum" of undeveloped thinking from appearing before the public and enabling authors to hold up a true mirror to the society they live in. These two sets of concerns, which I enlarge upon in the following, reflect the dual nature of internal rhetoric (also implicit in Isocrates) as both an ethical practice in its own right and an inventional strategy for public rhetoric.

Shaftesbury sees two primary personal goals for the individual engaging in internal rhetoric. The first, reflecting Shaftesbury's Stoic personal philosophy, is to attain consistency of character:

> This operation is for no inconsiderable end, since 'tis to gain him a Will, and ensure him a certain resolution, by which he shall know where to find himself; be sure of his own meaning and design; and as to all his desires, opinions, and inclinations, be warranted one and the same person to-day as yesterday, and to-morrow as to-day. (123)

The key to being the same person at all times is to be governed by reason rather than the emotions or appetites, which are constantly directed toward different objects.[17] Without such control of reason, a person could only be a "madman" (207). It is only by being thus consistent that we can know ourselves:

> 'Tis the known province of philosophy to teach us ourselves, keep us the self-same persons, and so regulate our governing fancies, passions,

> and humours, as to make us comprehensible to ourselves, and knowable by other features than those of a bare countenance. (184)

So for Shaftesbury, reason characterizes our true or "best" selves, while imagination, emotion, and the appetites are best treated as external to our true selves: "Fancy and I are not all one. The disagreement makes me my own" (209). In this, Shaftesbury sees himself as participating in a classical tradition stretching back to Socrates, and he claims ancient precedent for the necessity of dividing oneself to allow reason to stand as the "commanding genius" (128).

Shaftesbury departs from the classical tradition in the second personal purpose he gives for internal rhetoric, the discovery of one's goals. Aristotle, for example, argues that we deliberate only about means and not ends, because our ends are determined by our societal function or position (*Nichomachean Ethics* 1112b 12–16). For Shaftesbury, our goals are not that clear-cut:

> One would think there was nothing easier for us than to know our own minds, and understand what our main scope was; what we plainly drove at, and what we proposed to ourselves, as our end, in every occurrence of our lives. But our thoughts have generally such an obscure implicit language, that 'tis the hardest thing in the world to make them speak out distinctly. (113)

We hardly know what we think unless we query ourselves closely about it, and so likewise must we determine our goals in life. An important aspect of internal rhetoric, for Shaftesbury, is thus the "sincere consideration of my scope and end" (193). Internal rhetoric does not just manage emotions, then, but enables self-knowledge as well as self-definition: it has, in other words, an epistemic function. This is an important point in understanding Shaftesbury's practical philosophy of internal rhetoric, because without this added layer of complexity his descriptions of internal rhetoric appear as stringently rationalistic as Plato's and Aristotle's.

So Shaftesbury's version of internal rhetoric consists not only of allowing reason to take the part of the "preceptor" but of discovering where reason lies in our own confusing thoughts. The goal of such an exercise is "to get an aim, and know certainly where my happiness and advantage lies" (199). This is not an individualistic ethic, however, because Shaftesbury argues that "self affections," in a properly balanced "soul or temper," are necessary for "natural [i.e., social] affection":[18]

> The affections towards private good become necessary and essential to goodness. For though no creature can be called good or virtuous merely for possessing these affections, yet since it is impossible that the public good or good of the system can be preserved without them, it follows that a creature really wanting in them is in reality wanting in some degree to goodness and natural rectitude, and may thus be esteemed vicious and defective. (*Concerning Virtue* in *Characteristics* 1:288)

For Shaftesbury, there is no conflict between personal and social interests (*Concerning Virtue* in *Characteristics* 1:281–82). Internal rhetoric is thus an aid in attaining the harmony and proportion for an individual in relation to society and nature that for Shaftesbury constitutes the moral life.

While Shaftesbury sees the personal goals of internal rhetoric as most important, he also promises results that will professionally benefit his addressed audience of authors. He opens *Soliloquy* by commenting on how difficult it is to give anyone good advice without seeming self-serving, and that this is particularly true for authors because they are the "professed masters of understanding to the age" (104). His initial reason for introducing the topic of internal rhetoric, then, is to enable authors to practice giving advice to themselves before they impose on other people.

Shaftesbury is writing in quite a lighthearted vein in his introduction, as he is with his second goal of internal rhetoric, which is to keep authors from airing their "froth and scum in public" (108).[19] He compares the practice of publishing meditations and reflections to "taking . . . physic" or begetting children in public (109). He says, of these prematurely publishing authors, that they cannot practice internal rhetoric because they are never alone:

> For so public-spirited they are, that they can never afford themselves the least time to think in private for their own particular benefit and use. . . . They have their author-character in view, and are always considering how this or that thought would serve to complete some set of contemplations, or furnish out the commonplace book from whence these treasured riches are to flow in plenty on the necessitous world. (109)

Although Shaftesbury is clearly being satirical in this passage, his complaint offers a serious consideration for this history of internal rhetoric. For the first time, the explicit possibility of an internalized societal audience is raised—and immediately rejected.

Anticipating Rousseau, Shaftesbury does not have a high regard for the influence of society on people's morals (even though "social affection" is the major motivation for virtue):

> As to . . . the wrong sense or false imagination of right and wrong. This can proceed only from the force of custom and education in opposition to Nature, as may be noted in those countries where, according to custom or politic institution, certain actions naturally foul and odious are repeatedly viewed with applause, and honour ascribed to them. (*Concerning Virtue* in *Characteristics* 1:261)[20]

Instead, Shaftesbury is a Platonist who believes that people are endowed with an innate capacity for virtue that must be developed in accordance with a "fixed standard" of virtue and reason. Thus, an internalized audience representing the demands of society would not be welcome in an exercise whose purpose is to develop the natural moral sense and taste. Shaftesbury explains that this internalized societal audience is why a variety of language users—writers of memoirs, essays, and devout exercises; lovers; and "common great talkers" (111)—are unable to converse with themselves in a wholly private voice, and he suggests that only philosophers truly practice this "powerful figure of inward rhetoric" (123).

Shaftesbury asserts a more serious professional purpose for internal rhetoric than the private release of logorrhea. He suggests that the practice of internal rhetoric develops the reasoning capability of authors by "exercising their own genius so as to make acquaintance with it or prove its strength" (109). Shaftesbury thus sees internal rhetoric as a prerequisite, an inventional aid, for any kind of reasonable public discourse:

> His [an author's] thoughts can never appear very correct, unless they have been used to sound correction by themselves, and been well formed and disciplined before they are brought into the field. 'Tis the hardest thing in the world to be a good thinker without being a strong self-examiner and thorough-paced dialogist in this solitary way. (112)

Shaftesbury thus sees internal rhetoric as necessarily preceding public rhetoric. For Shaftesbury, then, internal rhetoric averts "uncontrollable harangues and reasonings" in public in two ways: by serving as a pressure valve for all the verbal "crudities, indigestions, choler, bile, and particularly . . . a certain tumour or flatulency" (111) that build up in people, and by enabling writers to practice reasoning correctly before they reason in public.

Shaftesbury's most serious goal for professional internal rhetoric also has to do with its function as a preliminary for public discourse: Internal rhetoric enables a writer to reflect universal truths by "deliberately" framing taste "by the just standard of nature" (228). Writers must learn to portray character by observing the "several motions, counterpoises and balances of the mind and passions" in themselves through internal rhetoric (126). Shaftesbury's models for "true poets" are Plato and Homer, in contrast to the "insipid race of mortals" who pass as poets during his time "for having attained the chiming faculty of a language, with an injudicious random use of wit and fancy" (135).[21] Shaftesbury uses the metaphor of the poet as a "second Maker" to describe his ideal:

> He notes the boundaries of the passions, and knows their exact tones and measures; by which he justly represents them, marks the sublime of sentiments and action, and distinguishes the beautiful from the deformed, the amiable from the odious. The moral artist who can thus imitate the Creator, and is thus knowing in the inward form and structure of his fellow-creature, will hardly, I presume, be found unknowing in himself, or at a loss in those numbers which make the harmony of the mind. (136)

Internal rhetoric enables knowledge of the self, which in turn enables the artist to portray the universal characteristics of human passions both in the harmony of virtue and in the unbalanced state that for Shaftesbury represents degeneracy: "for knavery is mere dissonance and disproportion" (136). Moreover, the balanced state of virtue promoted by internal rhetoric enables the poet to work toward "the real beauty of composition, the unity of design, the truth of characters, and the just imitation of Nature in each particular" (158). Thus, while Shaftesbury opens his treatise with a lighthearted approach to internal rhetoric, he finally claims that the exercise of "self-discourse" has a very serious aesthetic and moral purpose.

The fact that Shaftesbury begins his treatise in such a lighthearted vein indicates that he has a very different purpose in mind from Bacon. Except for his highly rhetorical addresses to King James I throughout book 1 of the *Advancement of Learning* and at the opening of each book thereafter, Bacon uses a plain style of writing, befitting his project to methodically transmit scientific knowledge. Shaftesbury is up to something very different, as evidenced in the various quotations cited above. He jokes, tells stories, and uses numerous extended metaphors and synonyms for what I have been calling internal rhetoric. In fact, Adam Smith, lecturing almost forty years later, blames Shaftesbury for falling into the "dungeon of metaphorical obscurity" (*Lectures on Rhetoric* 8). Instead of dismissing Shaftesbury as one of those authors who use "the chiming faculty of a language, with an injudicious random use of wit and fancy" (Smith, *Lectures* 135), though, I maintain that Shaftesbury's style reflects his own purpose in writing *Soliloquy.*

Since Shaftesbury believes that moral philosophy must have practical application, his writing embodies an unabashedly rhetorical attempt to change people's behavior and values.[22] As Robert Markley notes, Shaftesbury "sees 'philosophy' as a strategic and polemical discourse designed to inculcate in his readers a decidedly aristocratic sense of virtue" (141). Shaftesbury argues that the plain style of "super-speculative philosophy" is not practical writing, because even the leaders of that school have not learned how to regulate their own lives by their formal treatment of the passions (189–90). Shaftesbury, on the other hand, is trying to persuade his audience of authors to practice internal rhetoric so they can improve the quality of literature and thus of society. In doing so, he agrees with Bacon's critique of the Stoic attempt to teach ethics in unadorned prose (discussed above). So even though Shaftesbury has the same goal as the Stoics, to be ruled by reason at all times, his colorful style demonstrates he recognizes that the rhetorical task of moral philosophy requires nonlogical as well as logical appeals. Shaftesbury is not only describing the process of internal rhetoric, as Bacon does, but using vivid linguistic ornamentation to persuade his audience to practice it.[23]

Persuasion is not only needed to disseminate moral philosophy and the moral practice of internal rhetoric; it is also essential to the propagation of knowledge:

> Where persuasion was the chief means of guiding the society; where the people were to be convinced before they acted; there elocution became considerable, there orators and bards were heard, and the chief geniuses and sages of the nation betook themselves to the study of those arts by which the people were rendered more treatable in a way of reason and understanding, and more subject to be led by men of science and erudition. (155)

For Shaftesbury, as for Bacon, reason is the guiding principle of both internal and public rhetoric, and the vividness with which it is supported allows reason to overcome the importunities of the appetites and emotions. Shaftesbury thus wants his treatise to be a vivifying mirror to his age, giving his thoughts "voice and accent" (113) for the public in the same way that he does for himself in his private "self-discoursing practice."

Shaftesbury has provided a number of further considerations for my history of internal rhetoric. He offers a model of direct address between reason and the appetites that is distinctly rhetorical, although more agonistic than previous constructs. Thus, while he follows Plato and Aristotle in insisting on the dominance of reason over the misleading appetites, he maintains a rhetorical model for the governance of reason similar to Bacon's, as opposed to a coercive or "natural" dominance model. Shaftesbury is also Platonic in positing innate faculties and an innate (but corruptible) sense of the good, but he differs from Plato by arguing that the innate moral sense must be developed through internal rhetoric. Furthermore, Shaftesbury at least raises the question of whether internalized social voices participate—or should participate—in internal rhetoric, a construction that will become dominant in the twentieth century.

Shaftesbury also emphasizes the importance of internal rhetoric for moral and intellectual development and practice. Like Bacon, he chides those who attempt to inculcate moral teachings through unembellished language or logic, arguing instead that moral precepts should be made useful and attractive to one's audience through rhetorical means. He does not emphasize this particular claim for internal rhetoric as much as Bacon does, but reflects this precept in his own highly embellished writing style. Shaftesbury considers his style of philosophical writing to be quite practical, even though later critics like Adam Smith accuse him of pomposity abstracted from any appropriateness to himself or his subject matter (*Lectures on Rheto-*

ric 56, 58–89). Shaftesbury, then, is something of an anomaly compared with other philosophers later in the century, not only in his embellished style but also in various aspects of his philosophy that fail to reflect the theological and philosophical trends before and after him. The peculiarity most pertinent to a history of internal rhetoric is his simultaneous assertions of both the invidiousness of the passions, a Platonic viewpoint previously seen as detrimental to a theory of internal rhetoric, and the ethical need for internal rhetoric.

Of course, Bacon and Shaftesbury represent a small, elite male section of the population in one small nation. By this time in history, women are also publishing texts that address concerns related to internal rhetoric. Mary Astell, for example, is primarily known for her writings on women's education, in which she often mentions conversing with oneself as the means of self-discipline.[24] In *A Serious Proposal to the Ladies Part II: Wherein a Method is offer'd for the Improvement of their Minds* (1697), she writes:

> When the Will comes to ask the Understanding this Question, What must I do to fill up my Vacuities, to accomplish my Nature? Our Reason is at first too weak, and afterwards too often too much sophisticated to return a proper Answer, tho it be the most important concern of our Lives, for according as the Understanding replies to it so is the Moral Conduct of the Will, pure and right if the first be well Inform'd, irregular and vitious if the other be weak and deluded. (63)[25]

Astell writes from a faculty psychological viewpoint similar to Bacon's and Shaftesbury's. Like Bacon, she sees that moral discipline is a matter of making future goods more present to the imagination than sensory pleasures: "We shou'd endeavor to render Spiritual and Future things as Present and Familiar as may be, and to withdraw as much as we can from sensible Impressions" (143). Like Shaftesbury, she argues that we know other people by "looking into our own Hearts, one Person being but the Counterpart of another" (142; cf. *Soliloquy* 136): People are, at base, the same. She also anticipates Shaftesbury's claim that the passions inhibit internal rhetoric, writing that too much "Mirth" or "Melancholy" "rend[ers] us unfit to Converse with our selves" (141). Indeed, Astell condenses the whole issue of the relation of reason to the emotions into a pithy chiasmus: "It were better indeed . . . that the Passions did not move the Mind, but the Mind the Passions" (147).

It is significant that Astell writes in terms similar to those of Bacon and Shaftesbury, because she rejects the dominant, masculinist gendering of the faculties, arguing instead that women's reasoning powers are as strong as men's (Sutherland 107). Shaftesbury exemplifies exactly the traditional association of women with the emotions against which Astell is fighting:

> Nor is there anything ungallant in the manner of thus questioning the lady fancies, which present themselves as charmingly dressed as possible to solicit their cause. . . . It may be justly said of these, that they are very powerful solicitresses. (202)

It is therefore unlikely that Shaftesbury includes women when he asserts the equality of human souls, while Astell's appeal to the equality of all people not only includes women but is also addressed to women. Mary Wollstonecraft will also argue that men's and women's moral makeup is the same but for the corrupting influence of masculine society's demands on women—an ironic footnote to Shaftesbury's belief in the corrupting influence of society.

The intense interest in ethics, psychology, and rhetoric that characterizes Bacon, Astell, and Shaftesbury continues, but little attention is paid to their confluence in internal rhetoric through the rest of the eighteenth century. A brief outline of philosophical and rhetorical movements during this period will clarify the intellectual conditions necessary for maintaining a faculty psychological view of internal rhetoric.

The Eighteenth-Century Hiatus

What becomes evident in the typical intellectual histories of the eighteenth century is that internal rhetoric does not fit neatly into any of the theological, ethical, psychological, epistemological, or rhetorical debates that usually organize discussions of this period. I can illustrate this observation by comparing the two philosophers already discussed at length in this chapter, Bacon and Shaftesbury. Bacon is an orthodox Anglican, anxious to reconcile his scientific goals with Christianity, while Shaftesbury is a deist and skeptic.[26] Bacon ties ethics closely to theology and attributes to both reason and the imagination the guidance of moral choices, while Shaftesbury adheres to a Stoic philosophy that ties ethics solely to reason and to an innate moral sense and that deprecates the emotions.[27] Bacon argues that all human knowledge is obtained through observation; Shaftesbury believes that people have, if not innate knowledge, then innate predilections toward morality and beauty.[28] Bacon differentiates the knowledge attainable through observation from that only recalled by rhetorical invention,[29] while Shaftesbury argues that we cannot know our own minds, goals, or selves except through internal rhetoric. While both philosophers present strong depictions of internal rhetoric, then, their intellectual frameworks for internal rhetoric are quite different.

Bacon and Shaftesbury both have strong philosophical legacies in the eighteenth century; Bacon fosters empirical studies into human (as well as extrahuman) nature and Shaftesbury founds the moral sense school of philosophy. It is surprising, then, that neither tradition continues to see internal rhetoric as a phenomenon to be investigated. To account for the submergence of internal rhetoric during the eighteenth century, I focus on how various philosophers treat characteristic concerns of previous accounts of internal rhetoric that I have examined: namely, the relationship between the faculties (primarily reason, the emotions, and the will or motive faculty) and the nature and source of ethical action.

In the first place, a minimal possibility of faculty interaction is necessary for internal rhetoric to take place. John Locke denies the possibility of faculty interaction that has so far provided the locus of internal rhetoric, even though his "empirical" investigation of human understanding appears remarkably like Shaftesbury's rhetorical process of gaining self-knowledge.[30] Locke's interests are epistemological rather than ethical. His goal is to provide an "Account of the Ways, whereby our Understandings come to attain those Notions of Things we have" (44).[31] Psychologists following Locke may not deny the possibility of faculty interaction as he does, but they certainly do not account for it either, preferring to discuss the faculties more in terms of how they are affected by external influences than by internal, linguistic interactions. An example of this later associationist psychology is found in David Hartley, who argues that all of the faculties are generated by differing associations of vibrations impinging on the brain through the five senses. Hartley draws on Newton's theory of vibrations to explain the connection between the physical senses and mental sense perception, and he uses the doctrine of association (generally common to Hobbes, Locke, and Hume, among others) to explain all mental activities on the basis of those vibrations.[32] Hartley asserts that "our Passions or Affections can be no more than Aggregates of simple Ideas united by Association" (368) and that those associations are traceable to the vibrations made by the original sense impressions. Such accounts do little to forward a theory of internal rhetoric because they ignore the nature of thought as linguistically interactive in favor of a mechanistic, perceptual description of epistemic thought processes.

Like Mary Astell, Mary Wollstonecraft echoes the psychological precepts of her male peers while making the radical claim that women's minds work the same way men's do—by nature, although not by socialization. She too adheres to an associationist psychology to explain psychological development: "So ductile is the understanding, and yet so stubborn, that the associations which depend on adventitious circumstances, during the period that the body takes to arrive at maturity, can seldom be disentangled by reason. One idea calls up another, its old associate" (*A Vindication of the Rights of Woman* 248). At the same time, she uses associationism to explain the social differentiation between men and women:

> This habitual slavery, to first impressions, has a more baneful effect on the female than the male character, because business and other dry employments of the understanding, tend to deaden the feelings and break associations that do violence to reason. . . .
>
> [But for women] every thing that they see or hear serves to fix impressions, call forth emotions, and associate ideas, that give a sexual [i.e., feminine] character to the mind. (248-49)

According to Wollstonecraft, women are creatures of their emotions only because masculine society has not rewarded them for developing their intellects—or even allowed them to do so.[33] While all humans must strengthen the understanding through the exercise of "reflection and self-government" (150), women are prevented from doing so by the way society fosters emotionalism in them: "Their senses are inflamed, and their understandings neglected, consequently they become the prey of their senses, delicately termed sensibility, and are blown about by every momentary gust of feeling" (136). In these references to and depictions of moral reflection,

Wollstonecraft hints at a possible rhetorical interaction among the faculties without describing it explicitly.[34]

In addition to the possibility of intrapersonal linguistic interaction, a concept of internal rhetoric also requires the acknowledgment of a positive role for more than one faculty—typically, the emotions or the imagination in addition to reason—in making moral decisions and generating ethical action. If reason alone is seen to be capable of engendering or coercing ethical behavior as Plato and Aristotle argue, then internal rhetoric is either not necessary or actually an impediment to regulating human behavior.[35] Rhetorical theories of the eighteenth century typically express the need to address both the reason and the emotions of a public audience in order to move their collective will into action, but this same need to unify potentially diverse mental forces rhetorically is not recognized at the intrapersonal level by moral philosophers. Writers such as Thomas Reid, George Campbell, and Joseph Priestley acknowledge that orators must appeal to both reason and the emotions, but none of them extend that same rhetorical appeal to individuals controlling their own behavior. Reid, for example, argues that "all wisdom and virtue consist in following" the dictates of the "cool and rational" part of the mind (*Essays* 73). He distinguishes this "manly part of our constitution" from the brutish passions, which influence the will by force (*Essays* 71).[36] Public rhetoric, however, must appeal to both:

> With most men, the impulse of passion is more effectual than bare conviction; and, on this account, orators, who would persuade, find it necessary to address the passions, as well as to convince the understanding; and, in all systems of rhetoric, these two have been considered as different intentions of the orator, and to be accomplished by different means. (75)

In these passages, Reid reflects most of the components of the Baconian description of internal rhetoric—the interaction of reason and the emotions in public rhetoric, the inability of reason alone to move the will of a general audience, the necessity of moving the will to produce action—without more than implicitly recognizing the possibility of internal rhetoric.[37] So while Reid acknowledges the necessity of appealing to both reason and the emotions in public rhetoric, he does not extend that observation to an individual's self-control or self-knowledge. Moral philosophies that do not account for ethical judgments and actions in terms of the positive interaction of multiple faculties also generally fail to see a need for cultivating internal rhetoric toward making those decisions and initiating those actions.

It is not only philosophers who claim morality is governed by reason that ignore the potential for internal rhetoric, however. David Hume, for example, flatly denies that reason determines moral behavior:

> Nothing is more usual in philosophy, and even in common life, than to talk of the combat of passion and reason, to give the preference to reason, and to assert that men are only so far virtuous as they conform themselves to its dictates. . . . In order to shew the fallacy of all this philosophy, I shall endeavor to prove *first,* that reason alone can never be a motive to any action of the will; and *secondly,* that it can never oppose passion in the direction of the will. (*A Treatise of Human Nature* 413)

Both reason and the emotions have roles in moral choices, but not in a linguistically interactive manner; rather, the two faculties fulfill different functions in motivating behavior. Hume argues that reason plays only a mediating role in motivation, allowing us to determine the means for achieving some goal. Reasoning is the way we get from the desired effect to the causes that must be brought about to achieve it (*Treatise of Human Nature* 414). The goal itself, however, is always determined by the emotions or passions. Without the power to draw or repel us, an object cannot affect volition:

> Extinguish all the warm feelings and prepossessions in favour of virtue, and all disgust or aversion to vice: render men totally indifferent towards these distinctions; and morality is no longer a practical study, nor has any tendency to regulate our lives and actions. (*Enquiry Concerning the Principles of Morals* 172)

Hume, then, acknowledges both the affective and rational aspects of motivation and virtue without using a personified (or linguistically mediated) account of Reason and the Emotions. He does not raise the issue of whether the mind might need to negotiate means or ends using internal rhetoric, because reason and emotions do not seem to work jointly in arriving at either.

The rhetorics based on these new moral philosophies also tend to ignore or downplay the possibility of internal rhetoric.[38] Priestley does not treat an internal equivalent to public rhetoric, since his text is explicitly about public oratory, even though he follows Bacon by discussing appeals to the emotions in terms of stylistic ornamentation (71ff.). Campbell offers an interesting reason for excluding internal rhetoric from his theory of rhetoric. In his introduction, Campbell argues that the kind of internal interactions I have been characterizing as internal rhetoric are prior to the art of rhetoric, the raw material provided by nature on which we construct the rules of the formal art: "The earliest assistance and direction that can be obtained in the rhetorical art, by which men operate on the minds of others, arises from the consciousness a man has of what operates on his own mind" (lxxiv). This process is "supplied by Nature" rather than part of "the rhetorical art," however (lxxv). Thus, in the body of *The Philosophy of Rhetoric,* Campbell discusses public rhetoric only, even though he draws on faculty psychology and Bacon (lxxiii, 72) and cites as one of his purposes for the book the intent "to exhibit, he does not say, a correct map, but a tolerable sketch of the human mind" (lxvii).

Although British philosophers and rhetoricians in the eighteenth century preferred other explanations for the mental phenomena I have been examining, the history of faculty psychology and internal rhetoric does not end here. Internal rhetoric does not disappear completely as a presumption from eighteenth-century thought, and it emerges again as an object of theorizing in the rhetorical, psychological, and moral works of Richard Whately. Whately uses many of the same sources and arguments as his eighteenth-century counterparts, but returns to a concept of internal rhetoric to defend rhetorical appeals to the emotions.

Whately and Internal Rhetoric of the Passions

Given that reason dominates discussions and portrayals of internal rhetoric in the seventeenth and early eighteenth centuries, it is not surprising that in reaction, an alternative view arises that gives the emotions a legitimate role in ethically directed internal rhetoric. What may be surprising, however, is that this view should be promulgated by Richard Whately, a scholar known more for his Aristotelean logic and logic-based rhetoric than for being a champion of the emotions. Although he clearly perceives logic and empirical observation to be the bases for knowledge, he also argues that emotionally directed internal persuasion is necessary for ethical mental discipline, drawing on both Francis Bacon and Scottish moral sense philosophers such as Adam Smith and Dugald Stewart. In the *Elements of Rhetoric* he uses this depiction of internal rhetoric to justify the use of *pathos* in public rhetoric, but he also finds it important enough to repeat three decades later in *Introductory Lessons on Morals* (1857) and *Introductory Lessons on Mind* (1859) in the context of promoting moral self-discipline. For Whately, managing the emotions through internal rhetoric does not mean suppressing them, as it had for Bacon and Shaftesbury, but directing and sometimes even heightening them.

Before I discuss Whately's passage on internal rhetoric in the beginning of part 2 of the *Elements of Rhetoric,* I would like to situate that discussion in a larger picture of how Whately views rhetoric and language. First of all, Whately claims that the most important function of language for human beings (as opposed to "Brutes") is "as an *instrument of thought,*—a system of General-Signs, without which the Reasoning-process could not be conducted" (20).[39] He divides linguistic thought traditionally, between the functions of clarification and persuasion: "Reasoning may be considered as applicable to two purposes, which I ventured to designate respectively by the terms 'Inferring,' and 'Proving'; *i.e.* the *ascertainment* of the truth by investigation, and the *establishment* of it to the satisfaction of *another*" (5). Whately assigns to logic and experimentation the task of discovering the truth, a function that must be performed prior to rhetorical advocacy of the truth: "The process of *investigation* must be supposed completed, and certain conclusions arrived at by that process, *before* he begins to impart his ideas to others" (5). Thus, as many scholars have noted, Whately strips rhetoric of any epistemic function and assigns it a purely managerial role.[40] This same observation holds whether Whately is discussing public language or the language of thought:

> When I remarked . . . that it is a common fault, for those engaged in Philosophical and Theological inquiries, to forget their own peculiar office, and assume that of the Advocate, improperly, this caution is to be understood as applicable to the process of *forming their own opinions.* (5)

Whately is not arguing that people should never play the advocate to themselves. He is only saying that such advocacy cannot take the place of "candid [logical and empirical] investigation" (6). Once this initial truth-finding stage is over, then Whately, like Bacon, asserts the crucial nature of affective persuasion—of both the self and others. It is this second step, which opens part 2 ("The Address to the Will, or Persuasion") of the *Elements of Rhetoric,* that I focus on in the following. In order to fully distinguish Whately's passionate form of internal rhetoric from the previously discussed reason-based internal rhetorics, I begin by situating Whately's discussion of *pathos* in the context of moral sense philosophy.

Whately defends the use of emotional appeals in public rhetoric by arguing that "there can be no Persuasion without an address to the Passions" (176–77). Like Campbell, he claims that persuading the emotions is necessary to establish or reinforce the desirability of the proposed judgment or action (the end), while arguments to the understanding are used to convince auditors that the means proposed are "conducive to the attainment of that object" (175).[41] For this reason, Whately rejects "Prejudice existing against excitement of Feelings," noting that *pathos* "is usually stigmatized as 'an appeal to the Passions instead of the Reason'; as if Reason alone could ever influence the Will, and operate as a motive" (180).[42] Instead of dichotomizing reason and the emotions, Whately distinguishes between "improper appeals to the Passions" and the necessity of exciting "rational and *rightly directed*" emotions (180).

Whately is a little indecisive about how emotions are "rightly directed." On the one hand, he argues that the determination of "truth" through a reasoning process must take place prior to any emotional engagement. On the other hand, he places his moral and psychological assumptions under the rubric of Scottish moral sense philosophy, which posits a "*Moral-faculty,* called by some writers Conscience, by others Conscientiousness, and by Dr. A. Smith, the sense of Propriety" (187). He specifically cites Adam Smith and Dugald Stewart, who both argue that morality is based on an immediate perception of right and wrong—although neither reify this perception into a distinct moral sense.[43] Whately, however, argues that the moral sense is an innate human faculty like reason (*Lessons on Morals* 3–4). This moral sense exists prior to any societal intervention, since both civil law and Christian Scriptures assume that people have a "natural notion of moral right and wrong" and neither law nor Scripture is "designed to supply a complete set of precise rules as to every part of our conduct" (*Lessons on Morals* 5). Whately realizes, of course, that this "natural notion" can be cultivated or corrupted—just as reason can.[44] In this framework, the moral sense, rather than reason, is the ultimate arbiter of what is right, and thus an important contributor to internal rhetoric.

The positing of a separate moral sense does not mean that it operates in opposition to reason, but that they fulfill different functions in human moral life. Adam Smith, for example, gives this explanation for how reason relates to moral perception:

> Though reason is undoubtedly the source of the general rules of morality, and of all the moral judgments which we form by means of them; it is altogether absurd and unintelligible to suppose that the first perceptions of right and wrong can be derived from reason. (*Theory of Moral Sentiments* 320)

For Smith, as for the other moral sense philosophers (including Shaftesbury), people have an immediate perception of moral qualities, which is then subject to ratiocination. Whately, too, acknowledges that reason plays a role in ethics, albeit one subordinate to the moral sense: "The Sentiment of *Justice* [or the *Moral-faculty,* or *Conscience,* or *Conscientiousness,* or Sense-of-*Duty*] . . . needs the guidance and control of right Reason to guard against many mistakes that may arise" (*Lessons on Mind* 150).[45] He claims that conscience is "a kind of absolute Sovereign of the Mind" that nonetheless should "command the services of Reason, and inquire by the aid of that, *how* to act in the best manner" (*Lessons on Mind* 151).

This depiction of the rhetorical negotiations between reason and the moral faculty reflects the same kind of means-ends connection discussed earlier with regard to rhetorical appeals—but it also seems to contradict Whately's assertion in the beginning of the *Elements of Rhetoric* that truth is arrived at by reason before the emotions can be engaged in its support. If "right" and "wrong" are as objectively determined as physical facts—as Whately seems to think they are—then he has left a critical ambiguity at the core of his moral theory and thus at the center of what I am calling his theory of internal rhetoric: Is reasoning the means we use to persuade people toward ends determined by the emotions or moral sense, or are emotional appeals the means we use to persuade people toward truths attained through pure reasoning?

Because the determination of what is right or desirable has to do with sentiment as well as reason, Whately points out that the goal of rhetoric sometimes might be to excite rather than to repress emotions:

> Not only in the case of Religion, but in many others also, a man will often wonder at, and be rather ashamed of, the coldness and languor of his own feelings, compared with what the occasion calls for: and even makes efforts to rouse in himself such emotions as he is conscious his reason would approve. (*Elements of Rhetoric* 181)

Whately thus opposes both the arhetorical mental interactions of Plato and Aristotle and the internal rhetorics depicted by Bacon and Shaftesbury, in which the goal is always to suppress the emotions and enhance the workings of reason. His goal is still to manipulate the emotions, but not to completely suppress them.[46]

With this purpose in mind, Whately must posit a different kind of interaction among the faculties than Bacon or Shaftesbury had. The latter two philosophers describe how reason could effectively control the will, with the necessary correlative that the passions would then be ineffective. Whately, on the other hand, argues that people should create the right emotions in themselves, but acknowledges the major difficulty in this endeavor: "The Feelings, Propensities, and Sentiments of our nature, are not, like the Intellectual Faculties, under the direct control of Volition" (181). People may believe themselves to be able to will appropriate emotions, he notes, but they are merely mistaking their belief in the approved emotion for the emotion itself (181).

Instead, Whately argues that a person can manipulate emotions in herself or others only by indirect means, just as involuntary physical processes of the body are controlled indirectly:

> It is in vain to form a Will to quicken or lower the circulation; but we may, by a voluntary act, swallow a medicine which will have that effect: and so also, though we cannot, by a *direct* effort of volition, excite or allay any Sentiment or Emotion, we may, by a voluntary act, fill the Understanding with such thoughts as shall operate on the Feelings. (182–83)

Thoughts, here, is a vague term, but it becomes evident that Whately is discussing affective mental images. He thus posits a mediating role for the imagination in controlling the emotions, as Bacon did, but with the purpose of fostering rather than overcoming emotion:

> By attentively studying and meditating on the history of some extraordinary Personage,—by contemplating and dwelling on his actions and sufferings,—his virtues and his wisdom,-and by calling on the Imagination to present a vivid picture of all that is related and referred to,—in this manner, we may at length succeed in kindling such feelings, suppose, of reverence, admiration, gratitude, love, hope, emulation, &c., as we were already prepared to acknowledge are suitable to the case. (183)

For Bacon, the role of the emotions in furthering ends approved by reason was only implicit in his description of the affective power of style. Whately makes this connection explicit; in some senses, then, he is undermining the strict distinction among the moral functions of faculties promulgated by earlier writers. In doing so, Whately is reminiscent of Isocrates, who argues that the study of moral exempla influences one's own behavior at the same time that it provides material for the persuasion of others.[47] Whately, then, makes explicit a new rationale—the inability to control the emotions by acts of will—for age-old prescriptions to read stirring prose or to use the imagination to reinforce moral precepts.

Whately has thus presented the control of the emotions in fairly standard moral terms, especially relating it to Christian meditation on the Bible,[48] before he goes back to his original discussion of persuasion. Whately waits to connect this internal manipulation of feelings to rhetoric until the end of the passage on *pathos:*

> Now in any process such as this, (which is exactly analogous to that of taking a medicine that is to operate on the involuntary bodily organs,) a process to which a man of well-regulated mind continually finds occasion to resort, he is precisely acting the part of a skilful orator, to himself; and that too, in respect of the very point to which the most invidious names are usually given, "the appeal to the feelings." (183)

Whately does not portray the faculties themselves as engaging in a rhetorical interaction. He uses them to explain how rhetoric acts reflexively on the moral agent. In this, he is closer to Locke's considering the faculties to be powers of an agential self than to Bacon's and Shaftesbury's portrayals of the faculties exerting rhetorical agency on one another. Whately's formulation leaves any question of agency attached to the person rather than to particular mental faculties.

Whately thus posits an ethical *art*—that is, intentional practice—of internal rhetoric, one that fosters the emotions that will draw a person toward the ends determined by the moral sense through means determined by reason. He, like Shaftesbury, also recognizes that there is an uncultivated internal rhetoric that often occurs in the psyche:

> A man is in danger—the more, in proportion to his abilities—of exercising on himself, when under the influence of some passion, a most pernicious oratorical power, by pleading the cause as it were, before himself, of that passion. (186)

Such an appeal describes the first half of the distinction that Whately makes between "improper appeals to the Passions" and "rational and *rightly directed*" emotions (180). For Whately, as for Shaftesbury, people without self-control are more likely to practice unethical internal rhetoric, "For, universally, men are but too apt to take more pains in justifying their propensities, than it would cost, to control them" (186). The double-edged sword with which the allegorical figure Rhetorica was pictured during the Renaissance thus persists in the internal rhetorics of Shaftesbury and Whately.

In accounting for both ethical and unethical internal rhetorics, Whately distinguishes between skill in using words and moral virtue.[49] In fact, Whately seems to believe that the two qualities potentially exist in inverse proportion to one another: Intentionally or not, verbally clever people are more likely to mislead themselves or others. He cautions:

> Most persons are fearful, even to excess, of being misled by the eloquence of another: but an ingenious reasoner ought to be especially fearful of his own. There is no one whom he is likely so much, and so hurtfully, to mislead as himself, if he be not sedulously on his guard against this self-deceit. (187)

Skill in both internal and external rhetorics, then, is separable from virtue and is potentially conducive to the undermining of virtue. For this reason, Whately specifically rejects the *vir bonum* ideal:

> If at least that man is to be accounted the most perfect orator who (as Cicero lays down) can speak the best and most persuasively on *any* question whatever that may arise, it may fairly be doubted whether a *first-rate man can be a first-rate orator.* (31)

This is because a person of "the most philosophical mind" will require more time for "the most scrupulous accuracy of investigation" than someone of more "superficial cleverness," so the latter may often make the better extemporaneous speaker (31). In the case of either internal or public rhetoric, then, rhetorical proficiency is no guarantor of moral or intellectual rectitude.

Nonetheless, Whately has described an ethical practice of internal rhetoric that excites the emotions toward goals prescribed by the moral sense. He calls the person who practices this version of internal rhetoric one "of well-regulated mind" (183), "good and wise" (186). Whately even draws attention to this passage in his preface while enumerating the benefits of rhetorical study:

> I may add, that I have in one place (Part II. ch. 1. §2.) pointed out an important part of the legitimate art of the orator, in respect of the minds of his hearers, as coinciding exactly with the practice of a wise and good man in respect of his own mind. (xli)

He also repeats similar descriptions of ethical internal rhetoric much later in his life, in the *Introductory Lessons on Morals* and *on Mind.* For Whately, internal rhetoric is an *instrument* of virtue—capable of being misused—rather than its necessary *cause.* So Whately associates virtue and wisdom with internal rhetoric, even though he cautions that both internal and public rhetorics may be diverted from moral ends.

Whately's discussions of self-persuasion demonstrate that the thread of internal rhetoric has not been completely lost after the rhetorical and ethical theories of the eighteenth century. He answers the debate about reason and the emotions with a functional division between logic and rhetoric that does not rule out the role of the emotions in moral deliberation. In other words, Whately sees a role for persuasion of the emotions as well as conviction of the understanding in both internal and public rhetoric. He thus disagrees with such moral philosophers as Thomas Reid, who considers moral judgments to be addressed only by reason as opposed to the reasonable and affective rhetoric we must use to persuade an audience of ordinary people. Whately does, however, argue that such internal manipulation of the emotions must be consonant with reason, because it may also be used to reinforce inappropriate passions rather than allay them. With such a caveat in mind, Whately still associates the practice of internal rhetoric with wisdom and virtue, even if he does not identify the two as strongly as does Isocrates.

In this chapter, I have added an additional layer to my historical sampling of internal rhetoric by examining texts growing out of the New Philosophy that started in England with Francis Bacon. I have built on the "internal conversation" model of thought established in the first chapter by looking at texts that describe the ethical decision-making process—the directing of the will—as a rhetorical interaction among the faculties. However, Whately's discussion of *pathos* introduces two instabilities in faculty psychology versions of internal rhetoric: his seeming inconsistency about whether the final arbiter of morality is reason or moral sentiment, and his refusal to attribute rhetorical agency to the faculties themselves. Ultimately, faculty psychology, with its innate, functionally distinct parts of the mind, does not provide a flexible enough framework for internal rhetoric.

I have not merely presented a straw man in this chapter, though, to be blown away entirely by the Freudian and post-Freudian psychologies of part two. We can still identify with portrayals of the self based on seeing the faculties as independent agents, as Bailey White's humorous depiction of her desolation at her doctor's retirement illustrates:

> When I got out to the waiting room, my legs wouldn't walk any farther. I sat down on the cracked vinyl sofa. All my body parts felt like lumps of lead. I tried to reason with them. I wheedled and pleaded. I told my uterus, "Don't worry, I'll find you a new doctor, a real gynecologist. Maybe a nice lady gynecologist, who understands the special needs of women." But my uterus had gone into a kind of blue funk and did not respond.
>
> I told my knees, "We'll get a joint specialist, an orthopedist who does laser surgery." But my knees just glared balefully into the distance. I felt a twinge of pain. . . .
>
> "And a therapist!" I told my brain, "a psychotherapist licensed by the state! He'll read all the magazines and keep up with the latest neuro-

> ses." But all my emotions just huddled in a sodden mass and sulked. (183–84)

White's story epitomizes both the foundational metaphor behind faculty psychology, that mental functions are as innate and discrete as body parts, and its survival in contemporary culture.

Further, these descriptions of faculty psychological internal rhetoric have pointed out the crucial distinction between internal rhetoric at its most ideal and the "illegitimate" internal rhetoric of the passions. I have established two areas of concern, that of cultivated internal rhetoric as moral reasoning and of uncultivated internal rhetoric as a habit that undermines the "natural" (i.e., ideal) psyche. These are not always easy to keep apart, and I continue the same intertwining of cultivated and what will come to be understood as primary internal rhetoric in part two, on the twentieth century. Many of the same characteristics I have described for internal rhetoric over the past two chapters will appear again in the following, but in more modern dress.

Part Two

Primary Internal Rhetoric: Constituting Rhetorical Selves

A sea change in psychological theory occurs between parts one and two of this book, mostly in the person of Sigmund Freud, who theorizes both the unconscious and the internalization of social mores as the superego.

Here we examine twentieth-century rhetorical and psychological perspectives on internal rhetoric and the linguistically constructed self. Chapter 3 specifically looks at two rhetorics that have broadened the province of rhetoric to include mental phenomena, that of Chaim Perelman and Lucie Olbrechts-Tyteca and that of Kenneth Burke. These rhetoricians are particularly applicable to contemporary concerns, since they base their accounts on depth psychology and antifoundationalist philosophy. They find Freud's strict hierarchy of unconscious over conscious motives troubling, however, and Burke explicitly moves beyond Freud's conception of the psyche toward the social construction of the self.

In chapter 4 I construct the rhetorical self, a continuously accumulating product of primary internal rhetoric, out of the psychologies of George Herbert Mead and Lev Vygotsky. Both reject Freud's emphasis on the unavailability of unconscious mental processes to consciousness and focus instead on the mental interaction among internalized social voices. Finally, in the conclusion I delineate the rhetorical self more fully and show how cultivated internal rhetoric can still be seen to operate as moral reasoning in the context of the rhetorical self.

3

The Twentieth Century: Internal Rhetoric after Freud

> Listen, he told himself. You better cut this out. This is very bad for you and for your work. Then himself said back to him, You listen, see? Because you are doing something very serious and I have to see you understand it all the time. I have to keep you straight in your head. Because if you are not absolutely straight in your head you have no right to do the things you do for all of them are crimes and no man has a right to take another man's life unless it is to prevent something worse happening to other people. So get it straight and do not lie to yourself.
>
> —Ernest Hemingway, *For Whom the Bell Tolls*

Just as Campbell, Whately, and other rhetoricians of earlier periods look to their contemporary psychologies to explain the way rhetoric works within the mind, Kenneth Burke and Chaim Perelman with Lucie Olbrechts-Tyteca also refer to the psychological underpinnings of their language theories—but because the study of the human mind has undergone a fundamental revolution, the import of such references changes dramatically. Pre-twentieth-century psychologies divided mental functions into discrete, innate faculties that interacted with one another and the world in clearly defined or prescribed ways. In the twentieth century, however, psychologies became more complex as the unconscious aspects of the mind began to be theorized. These newer ways of viewing the mind called into question the discrete mental functions and the ability to know one's own mind propounded by faculty psychologies.

In addition to complicating the way we view the mind and its development, twentieth-century psychologies such as those of Sigmund Freud and his followers also moved the study of internal rhetoric away from the rationalist and theological ethics of earlier periods. One of Freud's major contributions to psychology was a change in psychological value terms from virtue and vice to normal and abnormal, health and sickness. Freud, in other words, completed the separation of psychology from ethics and theology and allied it instead with medicine.[1] The secular study of the mind had begun to be separated from metaphysical explanations as early as Hobbes in the seventeenth century, peaking in the eighteenth century with David Hume, and then, according to at least one history of psychology, reaching its decisive divorce in the writings of Immanuel Kant.[2]

But many of the earlier philosophers who posited biological or materialist explanations for mental phenomena also tried to reconcile their theories with theological assertions of the immaterial soul. David Hartley, for example, closed the first volume of *Observations on Man* with a claim that his theory of vibrations and association neither opposed nor supported "the Immateriality of the Soul" (512)—an interesting assertion, since he associated all mental phenomena with vibrations generated by the physical senses. As the nineteenth century developed, theology became less of an assumption in these psychological rhetorics and more of a prescriptive model, as in Whately's suggestion that people meditate on the Scriptures to manipulate their emotions.

Because its psychological underpinnings have shifted away from a rationalist or theological ethics, rhetoric—particularly internal rhetoric—regains its status as an epistemic as well as an ethical tool, a way of attaining and testing knowledge as well as a way of making moral decisions and actions. The alternative to the cultivated internal rhetoric depicted as moral reasoning in part one is no longer an uncultivated, pernicious rhetoric of the passions; it is the pervasive, unconscious primary rhetoric that shapes our very selves. "Psychological rhetoric" means something very different in the twentieth century than it had in the eighteenth and nineteenth centuries.

Like the psychological rhetoricians of the eighteenth century, Chaim Perelman and Lucie Olbrechts-Tyteca and Kenneth Burke are concerned with how rhetoric operates on its audience, and they introduce internal rhetoric into their theories in this context. These later rhetoricians, however, use the terms of depth psychology, particularly the unconscious, to explain the workings of rhetoric on and in the mind. Perelman and Olbrechts-Tyteca use depth psychology to question what they see as a distorted perception of "self-deliberation," but then in turn question the failure of depth psychology to recognize the rhetorical nature of rationalization. Burke also has an ambiguous relationship to depth psychology, embracing it as an explanation of deceptive identifications, but also questioning its narrow view of rationalization. Burke goes beyond depth psychology, though, to explore the relations between social and internal rhetoric in shaping the mind. This chapter examines both the psychological and intratextual contexts of Perelman and Olbrechts-Tyteca's and Burke's accounts of internal rhetoric in order to establish the place of internal rhetoric in what are perhaps the latest attempts to formulate completely new systems of rhetorical theory.

Perelman and Olbrechts-Tyteca on Self-Deliberation

Perelman and Olbrechts-Tyteca trace a slightly different genealogy for their discussion of self-deliberation than that sketched in the previous chapters because, as classically trained philosophers, they see the history of deliberation as following the tradition of logic, "the art of thinking," rather than the rhetorical tradition. They reject the twin absolutisms of logic as the "art of thinking" and of the depth psychology that they use to undermine the claims of logic, asserting that each view of mental activity is unrealistic because it fails to take audience—and therefore the rhetorical nature of deliberation—into account.

Perelman and Olbrechts-Tyteca construct a history of self-deliberation through the logicians and philosophers who assert the definition of logic as *the* art of thinking, from Descartes and Pascal to John Stuart Mill and the French rhetorician A. E. Chaignet. They explain how these writers perceive the "universality" of logical deliberation:

> Because when a person is thinking, his mind would not be concerned with pleading or with seeking only those arguments that support a particular point of view, but would strive to assemble all arguments that seem to it to have some value, without suppressing any, and then, after weighing the pros and cons, would decide on what, to the best of its knowledge and belief, appears to be the most satisfactory solution. (41)

Philosophers disparage rhetoric as strenuously as they valorize logical deliberation, since in comparison "speech addressed to another is . . . simply appearance and illusion" (41). Logical reasoning is addressed to the self as a representative of the universal audience and is thus the ideal discourse, the paradigm against which rhetoric is found wanting.[3]

Perelman and Olbrechts-Tyteca deny this dichotomization between logical deliberation and rhetoric, maintaining instead that deliberation is only a "particular case" of argumentation (which they associate with rhetoric): "From our point of view, it is by analyzing argumentation addressed to others that we can best understand self-deliberation, and not vice versa" (41). The argumentative or rhetorical model of self-deliberation—which the authors clearly offer as a "terministic screen" rather than a reality claim[4]—allows Perelman and Olbrechts-Tyteca to avoid the "logic good/rhetoric bad" trap that limits discussions of deliberation from a more positivist philosophical perspective.

By approaching self-deliberation as a particular case of argumentation, Perelman and Olbrechts-Tyteca eliminate the dichotomy between internal deliberation and external rhetoric represented by the positivists against whom they position themselves.[5] In their view, self-deliberation takes the form of dialogical argumentation, as it has for so many of the philosophers and rhetoricians discussed in this book: "Even in the realm of inward deliberation, . . . a person must conceive of himself as divided into at least two interlocutors, two parties engaging in deliberation" (14). Since it is but a form of argumentation, self-deliberation has the same potential foibles as that other mistakenly privileged form, dialectic:[6]

> In self-deliberation, can we not indeed discern reflections corresponding to a discussion and others that are merely a search for arguments in support of a previously adopted position? Can we wholly rely on the sincerity of the deliberating subject to find out whether he is in quest of the best line of conduct or is pleading a case within himself? (42)

Just as they had, in an earlier discussion, questioned the disinterested nature of dialectic and the possible objectivity of normal discussion (39), Perelman and Olbrechts-Tyteca here question the possibility of impartial internal rhetoric. We cannot presume that self-deliberation is a sincere act of reason any more than we can presume that dialectic (in life) is carried on as a disinterested search for an absolute truth.

They explain this doubt by raising the complicating factor of the unconscious: "Depth psychology has taught us to distrust even that which seems unquestionable to our own consciousness" (42). That is, people cannot be certain whether their reasoning is objective or whether it rests on irrational but unconscious predilections. The positivists' claim that they can isolate rational deliberation from emotion depends on the subject's complete awareness of her own affective and rational faculties, a psychological state that is considered to be impossible in this post-Freudian era.

Perelman and Olbrechts-Tyteca use depth psychology to criticize the positivists' psychological absolutism in a way that reflects on the previous chapter's discussion of faculty psychology. They argue that positivists falsely assume a complete separation of the mental faculties: "The error is that of conceiving man as made up of a set of completely independent faculties" (47). This separation is the basis of the "traditional distinction between action on the mind and action on the will" (47) or between philosophical and rhetorical discourse. According to this bifurcated view of human psychology, philosophical and rhetorical discourses have opposite goals:

> In this perspective, whereas the task of the philosopher, inasmuch as he is addressing a particular audience, will be to silence this audience's particular passions in order to facilitate the "objective" consideration of the problems under discussion, the speaker aiming at a particular action, to be carried out at an opportune time, will, on the contrary, have to excite his audience so as to produce a sufficiently strong adherence, capable of overcoming both the unavoidable apathy and the forces acting in a direction divergent from that which is desired. (47)

This split between philosophical discourse acting on the reason and rhetorical discourse acting on the will has traditionally accompanied the esteem of the former and the denigration of the latter.

Perelman and Olbrechts-Tyteca argue that this dichotomization fosters a serious philosophical consequence, which "consists in removing all rational justification from action based on choice, and thus making the exercise of human freedom absurd" (47). That is, if reason is divorced from any motive for action, as the positivists maintain (because anything not subject to scientific verification is "purely subjective"), then "free will" becomes an exercise in random wish-fulfillment. The stakes in arguing for a rhetorically based view of human knowledge and action are no less than the ability of human beings to make rational choices concerning their actions in the world. Perelman and Olbrechts-Tyteca thus use their discussion of self-deliberation to raise questions about the positivist agenda at the very site where the encrowning of reason takes its most personal and yet most consequential form—self-deliberation or internal rhetoric.

The problem with raising the framework of depth psychology to critique the separation of reason from will, however, is that in some ways it is as absolutist as the positivist philosophy Perelman and Olbrechts-Tyteca are trying to supplant. While positivists associate sincerity of purpose with reason, psychoanalysts associate it with the unconscious. According to Freud, the real motivations for our actions lie in the "most primitive and survivalistic element of psychological beings, the *Id*" (D. Robinson 381). In a sense, then, Freudians are merely displacing psychological truth or reality from the faculty of reason to the realm of the unconscious. Neither absolutism is consistent with the argumentative model of self-deliberation that Perelman and Olbrechts-Tyteca develop. So while they use depth psychology to critique the positivists' view of deliberation, they disagree with psychoanalysts on their separation of reasoning—"real motives"—from rationalization.[7]

Perelman and Olbrechts-Tyteca criticize the psychoanalytic notion of rationalization as an unwarranted dismissal of certain types of deliberation, objecting that it is not a sufficiently rhetorical account of the deliberative process. They would like to reverse the psychoanalysts' pejorative use of the term *rationalization* by taking into account the rhetorical situation of deliberation:

> The psychologist will say that the motives given by the subject in explanation of his conduct are rationalizations if they differ from the real motives which caused him to act and of which the subject is unaware. We shall give a wider meaning to the term rationalization, regarding it as immaterial whether or not the subject is unaware of the real motives for his conduct. (42)

From a rhetorical point of view, the important question about deliberation is how effective its argumentation is, not whether motives are originary or not.

To illustrate that this claim is not as radical as it sounds, Perelman and Olbrechts-Tyteca give three examples of interpersonal rhetoric in which reasons are derived after a decision has been made. The first is a situation described in more "scientistic" terms by John Stuart Mill, in which an untrained magistrate is advised to make legal judgments without publicly explaining his reasoning. Perelman and Olbrechts-Tyteca connect this situation to rationalization while confirming the validity of the advice:

> If Lord Mansfield's advice here was good, this is because, after the governor had given his decision based on his sense of equity, his legally trained assistants could "rationalize" the decision by adducing reasons which did not occur to the governor and were more in accord with the controlling law than the reasons he would have given in support of his decision. . . . Strictly legal reasons are adduced only for the purpose of justifying the decision to another audience. (42–43)

Perelman and Olbrechts-Tyteca describe this situation as "the insertion of the conclusion into a technical framework" (43). In public rhetoric, then, highly formalized contexts (such as legal codes) often dictate the "rationalizations" or justifications that may be offered ex post facto for a decision.

But rationalizations fulfill other functions in interpersonal rhetoric, as their second and third examples illustrate. If the first illustration is drawn from judicial rhetoric, the second is from epideictic rhetoric in that a woman seconds a difficult decision made by her husband: "She puts order into his ideas, gives the decision its setting, and, in doing so, reinforces it" (43).[8] So rationalizations can also have the legitimate rhetorical function of reinforcing convictions, of strengthening resolution. The third example, drawn from political discourse, gives an instance in which the British government provided a justification of a previously announced decision to exile an African king (43–44). The reasons/rationalizations given did not influence the actual decision, but were intended to influence public opinion to be favorable to that decision.

Each of these three examples demonstrates how widely accepted it is that reasons presented in public rhetoric are governed by audience considerations rather than by the reasoning process that led the rhetor to the decision. Aristotle, for example, describes the function *(ergon)* of rhetoric as "concerned with the sort of things we debate and for which we do not have [other] arts and among such listeners as are not able to see many things all together or to reason from a distant starting point" (*The Rhetoric,* 1357a 1–4). In other words, a public audience may not necessarily be able to follow the close reasoning that Aristotle attributes to dialectic among philosophers, so they are given "after the fact" rhetorical proofs—rationalizations that will be more persuasive for them.

Perelman and Olbrechts-Tyteca draw on this acceptance of rhetorical proofs to give the same argumentative validity to reasons arrived at after a decision is made in self-deliberation. Because they consider self-deliberation a type of argumentation, the persuasive value they have illustrated in these examples of interpersonal "rationalizations" transfers to internal rhetoric:

> As appears from all we have just said about audiences, the rhetorical value of a statement is not, from our point of view, destroyed because the statement is predicated on argumentation thought to be elaborated after the inner decision has been made nor because it involves argumentation based on premises that the speaker himself does not accept. (44)

Perelman and Olbrechts-Tyteca, then, argue that successful self-deliberation must effect the same kind of persuasion as public rhetoric or argumentation: *"to induce or to increase the mind's adherence to the theses presented for its assent"* (4). The audience for internal rhetoric is both the person doing the deliberating and any eventual outside audiences to whom the matter of the deliberation might be presented: "This kind of rationalization is perfectly explained if we regard it as a pleading that is thought out in advance for the benefit of others, and can even be adapted to each particular anticipated audience" (42). Perelman and Olbrechts-Tyteca do not distinguish internal from external audiences, because the deliberator might be a member of the potential external audiences to whom the self-deliberation is addressed (44). In short, the deliberator is always a socially situated human being, not Descartes's "disembodied, unrelated, alone self" (Levin 8).

Perelman and Olbrechts-Tyteca's view of rationalization as a valid mode of self-deliberation is thus entailed by the audience-based thrust of their entire treatise on argumentation. *All* self-deliberation must be considered as reasoning for an audience of one sort or another, since the originating impulse toward a decision may not be available to consciousness. They are aware, however, that they must defend this view against people who want to be able to attribute "real" motives to an action or decision. In the case of rationalizations,

> The charge of insincerity or hypocrisy might be made by an observer or adversary. However, such an objection is significant only when made from a quite different standpoint than ours. Usually, moreover, the objector's perspective in such a case will be based on a well-defined conception of reality or personality. (44)

In other words, the search for "real" motives is based on the absolutist position that there is a single transcendent truth or reality. Their response to that claim reveals the epistemic significance of their theory of argumentation.

In answer to the absolutist view of truth and reality, Perelman and Olbrechts-Tyteca argue that both "fact" and "truth" are statuses attributed by a "community of minds" to constructs that the community is willing to treat as premises for argumentation. They thus explain how facts and truths are historically and culturally situated:

> From the standpoint of argumentation, we are confronted with a fact only if we can postulate uncontroverted, universal agreement with respect to it. But it follows that no statement can be assured of definitively enjoying this status, because the agreement can always be called into question later, and one of the parties to the debate may refuse to qualify his opponent's affirmation as a fact. Normally, there are thus two ways in which an event can lose the status of fact: either doubts may have been raised within the audience to which it was presented, or the audience may have been expanded through the addition of new members who are recognized as having the ability to judge the event and who will not grant that a fact is involved. (67)

Perelman and Olbrechts-Tyteca thus use the perspective of argumentation to explain how facts can differ from community to community and how, over time, they may be discarded as "true" and thus made subject to argumentation.[9] Their argument for an audience-based definition of "facts" and "truths" underlies their explanation of how rationalizations are socially situated, and it further undermines the logical view of deliberation, in which the deliberating subject seeks knowledge of an objective reality.

Value-laden distinctions between rationalizations and reasons or between logical deliberation and internal rhetoric are unrealistic in their isolation of reason from other facets of the mind and their search for unitary truths of mental acts. In contrast to this, Perelman and Olbrechts-Tyteca see their argumentative reading of self-deliberation as characteristic of an integrated, pragmatic, and volitional approach to the human world. Accordingly, "argumentation alone (of which deliberation constitutes a special case) allows us to understand our decisions" (47). Startlingly, although Perelman and Olbrechts-Tyteca specifically deny the rigid compartmentalization of the psyche evident in the faculty psychologies discussed in chapter 2, they arrive at a conclusion very similar to Bacon's: that rhetoric, particularly internal rhetoric, is an essential ingredient in the ethical aspects of human behavior.

In *The New Rhetoric,* then, Perelman and Olbrechts-Tyteca fight against the search for an absolute truth and its concomitant elevation of reason as the faculty for perceiving that truth—the positivists' attempt to make philosophy "scientific." They clearly assert that their position on argumentation is based on the refutation of such absolutist stands:

> We combat uncompromising and irreducible philosophical oppositions presented by all kinds of absolutism: dualisms of reason and imagination, of knowledge and opinion, of irrefutable self-evidence and deceptive will, of a universally accepted objectivity and an incommunicable subjectivity, of a reality binding on everybody and values that are purely individual. (510)

In all their criticisms of absolutist philosophies, Perelman and Olbrechts-Tyteca never make the paradoxical claim typically attributed to relativists that "everything is relative": rather, they demonstrate the consequences and implications of absolutist positions and argue that certain of the negative consequences can be avoided by viewing human phenomena from an argumentative standpoint. They thus reflexively enact the *rapprochement* between philosophy and rhetoric that they argue for in their introduction, since argumentation—the "*gaining* [of] *the adherence of minds*" (14)—is both their standpoint and their technique for a philosophical inquiry into human epistemology.

Kenneth Burke's Expansion of Rhetoric Inward

I now turn to the other great rhetorical system-builder of the twentieth century, Kenneth Burke. Like Perelman and Olbrechts-Tyteca, Burke has an ambivalent view of depth psychology, characterizing the Freudian psyche as profoundly rhetorical but critiquing the psychoanalytic view of rationalization. While Burke is not addressing a philosophical audience as Perelman and Olbrechts-Tyteca are, he also demonstrates how rhetorical motives are found in unexpected places. Burke's overall agenda is to reveal the "rhetorical motive" or function in all human endeavors, thus extending the "range"—and inevitability—of rhetoric to all forms of human communication and thought.

For Burke, rhetoric is *"rooted in an essential function of language itself . . . the use of language as a symbolic means of inducing cooperation in beings that by nature respond to symbols"* (*Rhetoric* 43). In his insistence that rhetoric and language, "symbolic action," are at the core of human cooperation and therefore social life, Burke brings to mind Isocrates' powerful and inclusive hymn to *logos:*

> Because there has been implanted in us the power to persuade each other and to make clear to each other whatever we desire, not only have we escaped the life of wild beasts, but we have come together and founded cities and made laws and invented arts; and, generally speaking, there is no institution devised by man which the power of speech *(logos)* has not helped us to establish. (*Nicocles,* §§5–7)

Isocrates thus anticipates Burke in recognizing the pervasiveness of rhetorical language use in human life, both holding exceptionally inclusive views for the mainstream of rhetorical history. Burke not only rejects any distinction between rhetorical and nonrhetorical uses of language in the world ("wherever there is 'meaning,' there is 'persuasion'" [*Rhetoric* 172]), but in doing so further undermines the descriptions of internal rhetoric constructed in part one, which depend on distinct, conscious roles for specific mental agencies such as those posited by faculty psychology or positivist philosophy.

To understand how Burke helps develop a theory of internal rhetoric and how internal rhetoric plays a significant role in Burke's language theory, I will analyze the section of *A Rhetoric of Motives* in which Burke discusses his extension of the "range of rhetoric" into mental processes. Burke views internal rhetoric initially through the psychological framework of Sigmund Freud, so I will follow him, briefly, to the Freudian theory that Burke uses to establish the rhetorical nature of the psyche. But Burke goes beyond Freud, developing the metaphor of the "parliament of the psyche" into a discussion of the internalization of social voices that has larger significance for internal rhetoric in Burke's theory of language and rhetoric. In closing, I will examine how Burke's discussion of internal rhetoric adds to my own growing theory, embodying a radical departure from the historical sense of internal rhetoric I have gathered so far, but also serving as a theoretical extension of the holistic Isocratean view of rhetoric that has been lost in the tussle over reason and the emotions that began with Plato and occupied the previous chapter.

Burke particularly emphasizes the transactional or relational nature of internal rhetoric by giving his section on "Rhetoric of 'Address' (to the Individual Soul)" a pivotal role in his discussions of "the two main aspects of rhetoric: its use of *identification* and its nature as *addressed*" (*Rhetoric* 45). Identification is relational because it occurs, or fails to occur, between two people or among a group of people: it always implies an individual or group identifying with another or others. Similarly, pointing out the "nature [of rhetoric] as *addressed*" underscores this relational quality, emphasizing that in their rhetorical nature, language and meaning are always to someone and for someone.

Like the rhetoricians and philosophers I have considered earlier, Burke is able to treat mental activity as fully rhetorical—that is, a linguistic, dialogical, and influential transaction between two or more entities—because he views the psyche as a heterogeneous entity. Burke fits the "Individual Soul" into this relational pattern of rhetoric by focusing not on "the individual in his uniqueness" (*Rhetoric* 37) but on psychologies that emphasize interactions between different factions of the personality. I examine the key role played by internal rhetoric in the construction of Burke's broad rhetorical theory by showing first how Burke's discussion of identification leads into the section on internal rhetoric and then how this passage in turn is used to introduce the "nature [of rhetoric] as *addressed*."

Burke uses the term *identification* as an "instrument" to show "how a rhetorical motive is often present where it is not usually recognized, or thought to belong" (*Rhetoric* xiii).[10] *Identification* is Burke's term for the way that language-users assert mutual interests or "consubstantiality" with their listeners (*Rhetoric* 20–21). Whereas persuasion implies a more unidirectional action—it is something a speaker does to her audience—identification encompasses the symbolic actions of both speaker and audience. Burke sees the two terms as being complementary ways of describing rhetorical language use:

> As for the relation between "identification" and "persuasion": we might well keep it in mind that a speaker persuades an audience by the use of stylistic identifications; his act of persuasion may be for the purpose of causing the audience to identify itself with the speaker's interests; and the speaker draws on identification of interests to establish rapport between himself and his audience. So, there is no chance of our keeping apart the meanings of persuasion, identification ("consubstantiality") and communication (the nature of rhetoric as "addressed"). But, in given instances, one or another of these elements may serve best for extending a line of analysis in some particular direction. (*Rhetoric* 46)

So identification, for Burke, is a particularly flexible way of describing the symbolic actions that occur in a rhetorical situation.

Burke also prefers to describe the function of rhetoric as identification rather than persuasion because identification emphasizes the positive connecting and cooperative aspects of language use over the "presence of strife, enmity, faction as a characteristic motive of rhetorical expression" (*Rhetoric* 20).[11] Persuasion, on the other hand, is often adversarial: "Since persuasion so often implies the presence or threat of an adversary, there is the 'agonistic' or competitive stress" (*Rhetoric* 52). Burke's preference for the term *identification* thus allows him to sidestep traditional, agonistic connotations of rhetoric and explore other ways that language and actions can be rhetorical. Among the many avenues of thought that the terministic screen of "identification" opens up for Burke is the possibility of unconscious identifications.

In the section titled "Ingenious and Cunning Identifications," Burke argues that rhetorical purposes may be unconscious as well as conscious, thus expanding and complicating the arena of internal as well as external rhetorical action. Burke explains how his conception of rhetoric goes beyond the conscious:

> There is a wide range of ways whereby the rhetorical motive, through the resources of identification, can operate without conscious direction by any particular agent. Classical rhetoric stresses the element of explicit design in rhetorical enterprise. But one can systematically ex-

> tend the range of rhetoric, if one studies the persuasiveness of false or inadequate terms which may not be directly imposed upon us from without by some skillful speaker, but which we impose on ourselves, in varying degrees of deliberateness and unawareness. (*Rhetoric* 35)

Burke thus acknowledges a spectrum of "degrees of deliberateness" for any rhetorical act, a gradated approach that differs from previous accounts of internal rhetoric. Burke eliminates the dichotomy between conscious and unconscious rhetorical motives that underlies delimited definitions of rhetoric such as George Campbell's distinction between the "art" of rhetoric and the "first impulse" toward it supplied by "Nature" (*The Philosophy of Rhetoric,* lines xxiv–xxv). Recognizing that rhetoric can be unconscious as well as conscious is not enough to fully explain the pervasiveness of the rhetorical motive in human life; rather, attending to variable levels of consciousness in rhetorical acts gives a more accurate sense of the way people persuade and are persuaded in everyday life.

By breaking down the dichotomy between conscious and unconscious rhetoric, Burke questions the strict association of unconscious or uncontrolled internal rhetoric with self-deception. Plato, Shaftesbury, and Whately all argue that without conscious control, internal rhetoric becomes a tool of the misleading emotions or passions, while Burke uses this unconscious-equals-false association only as a starting point for his exploration of internal rhetoric.[12] To get beyond that association, Burke recognizes the overdetermination of motive behind any rhetorical act:

> Whatever the falsity in overplaying a role, there may be honesty in the assuming of that role itself; and the overplaying may be but a translation into a different medium of communication, a way of amplifying a statement so that it carries better to a large or distant audience. (*Rhetoric* 36)

Burke has, in other contexts, pointed out at least two ways that motives vary in relation to any particular act. In *Permanence and Change,* he sees motives as interpretations of situations, which vary according to our operative worldview(s) (35). In *A Grammar of Motives,* Burke argues that how we define the circumference of scene in which an act takes place affects our interpretation of that act (77). Motives, then, are always multiple, and which motives are acknowledged may change, depending on their audience (including the self and its differing internal voices or attitudes). Value terms such as *deceptive* often relate to a simplistically defined rhetorical situation, seen as a completely conscious and intentional transaction. Burke argues that motives are never pure but always overdetermined and hence "deceitful" from some perspectives and "true" from others. According to Burke, we must qualify such labels in complex rhetorical situations as we understand the variety of purposes and effects that may occur simultaneously, consciously or not.

Burke's position on the multiplicity of motives puts him in full accord with Perelman and Olbrechts-Tyteca's analysis of rationalization. He makes a similar claim in *Permanence and Change,* where he criticizes the Freudian view of rationalization for its failure to recognize the situatedness of motivation:

> The term rationalization, as distinct from reasoning, seems to have come from psycho-analysis. As soon as the Freudians had developed their special terminology of motives, they felt the need of a term to characterize non-Freudian terminologies of motives. Thus, if a man who had been trained, implicitly and explicitly, in the psychological nomenclature fostered by the Church were to explain his actions by the use of this Church vocabulary, the Freudians signified a difference between his terms and their terms by calling theirs 'analysis' and his 'rationalization.' In general, he was thought to be concealing something from himself, especially if he put forward a noble or self-sacrificing set of terms to account for an act of his which the Freudian orientation could explain by a directly selfish motive. (17)

He goes on to observe, "Why this man should have been suspected of self-deception when using the only vocabulary of motives he had ever been taught, will remain one of the mysteries of psycho-analytic rationalization" (18). Burke's use of Freudian theory is thus not without reservation. He critiques the psychoanalytic view of rationalization as an unwarranted imperialism of terminology, while Perelman and Olbrechts-Tyteca critique it as a rhetorically simplistic view of deliberation.

His reservations about "rationalization" aside, Burke does use theories of the personality springing from the work of Sigmund Freud to expand the "range of rhetoric," and it is out of Freud's description of the psyche that he begins his analysis of internal rhetoric. Burke uses Freud's analysis of the psyche, just as earlier writers had used faculty psychology, to provide the mental factions necessary for a rhetorical examination of the self and its identifications. According to Freud, the personality is divided into three "psychical provinces or agencies" (*Outline* 145): the id, the original component of the psyche consisting of or containing the instincts and passions; the ego, a part of the id that developed to mediate between the desires of the id and the demands of the outside world; and the superego, the conscience or internalized voice of parental and societal norms.[13] These interacting factions of the mind provide the scene in which rhetoric takes place. The significance of this account is the strict separation Freud posits for the unconscious id, the workings of which are unavailable to the normal waking mind. Burke illustrates the complexities that depth psychology adds to a picture of internal rhetoric by analyzing three rhetorical situations that can occur within the psyche: the dream, the joke, and the psychological "parliament."

Dreams are important in Freudian theory because they are one of the few ways that the contents and associative patterns of the unconscious id become available to the normal (nonpsychotic) conscious mind.[14] Although Freud's descriptions of "dream work," the psychological process of dream formation, are typically complex, a brief sketch of the process is found in *An Outline of Psycho-Analysis:*

> Unconscious material from the id (originally unconscious and repressed unconscious alike) forces its way into the ego, becomes preconscious ['capable of becoming conscious' (160)] and, as a result of the ego's opposition, undergoes the changes which we know as *dream-distortion.* (165)

This sketchy description can be explained as follows. The id is the repository of both instincts and the unresolved psychic tensions that build up during the day (*Outline* 166). Because the id seeks to alleviate excitation in Freud's tension-reduction model of the psyche, these unresolved tensions exert pressure on the ego that threatens to disturb sleep. The ego tries to maintain sleep and get rid of the disturbance through wish-fulfillment, an apparent meeting of the demands of the id (*Outline* 169–70). Since the id is characterized by illogical associative patterns such as condensation, in which a single dream element may stand for many latent dream thoughts (*Outline* 167–68), and displacement, in which emotional intensity may be transferred from one object to another (*Outline* 168), the manifest dream may not be easily understood by the waking ego. In this explanation of dreams, language—symbolic action, in Burke's terms—acts in a complex way to coordinate the conflicting goals of the various components of the mind and to resolve the tensions generated by these conflicts.

To Burke, this explanation of dreams is a prime example of the characteristically human nature of the rhetorical motive:

> Indeed, what could be more profoundly rhetorical than Freud's notion of a dream that attains expression by stylistic subterfuges designed to evade the inhibitions of a moralistic censor? What is this but the exact analogue of the rhetorical devices of literature under political and theocratic censorship? The *ego* with its *id* confronts the *superego* much as an orator would confront a somewhat alien audience, whose susceptibilities he must flatter as a necessary step towards persuasion. (*Rhetoric* 37–38)

Burke here compares the distorting processes of dream work with two more traditionally recognized rhetorical situations: the rhetorical response of literature to the strictures of censorship and the case of an orator speaking before an unsympathetic audience. In each case, the message and desires of the rhetor must be made palatable to or identified with the conflicting desires and needs of the audience. The Freudian explanation of dream work reinforces the observations made earlier on the overdetermination of rhetorical motive. The message of the dream is translated into an esoteric symbol system that means one thing (avoidance of threatened loss of sleep) to the ego, which might be considered the immediate audience; another (release of excitation) to the id, the rhetor; and other possible interpretations for the reflective self or the psychotherapist, unintended audiences that may be considered eavesdroppers of dream rhetoric.

The next rhetorical situation that Burke draws from Freudian theory is that of the joke, citing Freud's *Wit and Its Relation to the Unconscious*. He is particularly interested in Freud's description of the rhetorical situation of tendentious jokes,[15] which Freud defines as those serving a purpose other than pure verbal enjoyment:

> Tendency-wit usually requires three persons. Besides the one who makes the wit there is a second person, who is taken as the object of the hostile or sexual aggression, and a third person in whom the purpose of the wit to produce pleasure is fulfilled. (*Wit* 695)

Freud describes the tendentious joke primarily as an external rhetorical situation, although he does explain the rhetoric of obscene jokes in terms of a missing, imagined female target of the joke (*Wit* 693).

Burke, again comparing internal with external rhetoric, focuses on the possibility of internalizing such a situation:

> In particular, we think of Freud's concern with the role of an audience, or "third person," with whom the speaker establishes rapport, in their common enterprise directed at the butt of tendentious witticisms. Here is the purest rhetorical pattern: speaker and hearer as partners in partisan jokes made at the expense of another. If you "internalize" such a variety of motives, so that the same person can participate somewhat in all three positions, you get a complex individual of many voices. (*Rhetoric* 38)

In this case, the act of internal rhetoric is shown to be complex in that a rhetor might have a variety of motives, possibly conflicting, for engaging in a single rhetorical act. Burke is once more complicating the internal rhetorical situation beyond a simple rhetor-audience model, for here he includes a secondary audience within the rhetorical situation, the target of the hostilities or aggressiveness, toward whom the rhetor has a different intent than toward the primary audience. Even the inclusion of hostile or aggressive motives in an internal rhetorical situation changes the nature of such a symbolic action, as it takes into account the "dark side"—what Jungians call the "shadow"—of the personality that earlier writers on internal rhetoric want to suppress.[16] So the analogy between internal rhetoric and the tendentious joke provides a model of internal rhetoric in which multiple audiences exist for the same (or each) rhetor, who might have a differing intent toward each audience.

Thus far I have shown how Burke uses the Freudian model of the psyche to add a number of complications to the earlier, relatively straightforward accounts of internal rhetoric. My previous depictions of internal rhetoric, based largely on faculty psychology, consisted of a conscious, motivationally pure (that is, either intentionally deceitful or truthful) act on the part of one aspect of the psyche directed toward another (singular) part of the psyche. Burke would have us view internal rhetoric as not wholly conscious, an act of overdetermined and possibly contradictory motivations and multiple audiences. The difference, Burke might argue, is that the internal rhetorical situation includes the conscious mind recognized by earlier philosophers as well as more or less unconscious mental processes, thus broadening the "scene," the frame of reference for that particular symbolic action.[17]

Burke also broadens the scene of his discussion of internal rhetoric by introducing the metaphor of a parliament for this intrapsychic rhetorical situation: "The Freudian psyche is quite a parliament, with conflicting interests expressed in ways variously designed to take the claims of rival factions into account" (*Rhetoric* 38).[18] The image is not a specifically Freudian one; it is used by Jungians like Erich Neumann to describe the balance of forces that is necessary for mental health:[19]

> Ego-consciousness becomes the locus of responsibility for a psychological League of Nations, to which various groups of states belong, primitive and prehuman as well as differentiated and modern, and in which atheistic and religious, instinctive and spiritual, destructive and constructive elements are represented in varying degrees and coexist with each other. (102)

The scene of internal rhetoric has thus been expanded again, from a single orator addressing a homogeneous but alien audience or multiple audiences with different purposes to a scene in which negotiation is taking place between any number of parties within the personality. There is no longer a distinct rhetor speaking to a known audience, as pictured by earlier faculty psychology accounts of internal rhetoric, but rather a number of factions within the psyche that may be taking the part of rhetor or audience in successive or simultaneous rhetorical acts. With multiple "rhetors" and multiple "audiences" representing diverse interests, the parliamentary image of internal rhetoric exponentially increases its complexity, obviating the dichotomy between deception and truth and implying instead the necessity and art of compromise. In the parliamentary mode, internal rhetoric is seen not as deceptive identification but as an act of negotiation, a means of compromise by which various conflicting needs or drives (such as the pleasure principle and the reality principle, for Freud) can be met.[20]

Burke has thus used Freudian psychology, with its fruitful concept of the unconscious within a multifaceted and overdetermined psyche, to complicate faculty psychology's concern with whether reason or the passions is the controlling rhetor in the psyche. The psychic parliament metaphor completes the move to seeing internal rhetoric as a complex system of symbolic interaction.

When analyzing the nature of the participants of this psychic parliament, Burke focuses on the role of the audience in internal rhetoric, thus introducing his second "main aspect" for exploring the breadth of rhetorical motive: "its nature as *addressed,* since persuasion implies an audience" (*Rhetoric* 38). Although he uses Freudian psychology to describe the internal rhetor's/rhetors' varying acts of identification and division, he moves away from a Freudian interpretation of the psyche into social psychology when he introduces his discussion of audience and the addressed nature of rhetoric:

> A man can be his own audience, insofar as he, even in his secret thoughts, cultivates certain ideas or images for the effect he hopes they may have upon him; he is here what Mead would call "an 'I' addressing its 'me' "; and in this respect he is being rhetorical quite as though he were using pleasant imagery to influence an outside audience rather than one within. (*Rhetoric* 38)

Burke here describes the same kind of imaginative internal *pathos* that I pointed out in Bacon and Whately, but with the vocabulary of George Herbert Mead's social psychology. Rather than emphasizing interactions between specific factions of the psyche, Burke presents a more reflexive view of internal rhetoric in discussing the nature of rhetoric as addressed. This perspective of the self as an audience for internal rhetoric enables Burke to bring out the "ingredient of rhetoric in all *socialization,* considered as a *moralizing* process" (*Rhetoric* 39)—his version of the cultivated internal rhetoric that was the central concern of internal rhetorics developed in part one.

Burke, then, also addresses the ethical nature of internal rhetoric, but more as a way of justifying behavior rather than promoting ethical decision making:

> A modern "post-Christian" rhetoric must also concern itself with the thought that, under the heading of appeal to audiences, would also be included any ideas or images privately addressed to the individual self for moralistic or incantatory purposes. For you become your own audience, in some respects a very lax one, in some respects very exacting, when you become involved in psychologically stylistic subterfuges for presenting your own case to yourself in sympathetic terms. (*Rhetoric* 38–39)

Burke's description of moralization is very different from the descriptions of moral reasoning I discussed in part one. Earlier philosophers who connected internal rhetoric with ethics had a defined theological or rationalistic framework within which they described the workings of internal rhetoric. Thus, thinkers such as Plato, Shaftesbury, and Whately saw reason or the moral sense having moral authority as the internal rhetor due to its perception of truth or its affinity to divine nature. Burke offers no such transcendent means of justification or authorization, but sees moralization as a kind of verbal legerdemain ("psychologically stylistic subterfuges") for an internal audience.[21] But while Burke substitutes the internal audience for any transcendent means of moral justification, he also recognizes the role of society in creating norms for human behavior.

Until Burke begins the discussion of socialization, his arguments about unconscious and internal rhetoric seem to refer only to an individual's internal persuasion, having little overlap with external or public rhetoric other than illustrative comparison. But stressing how a person can serve as her own audience allows Burke to posit a true intersection between internal and external rhetoric, not just a parallelism. The most private psychological phenomenon, as he has portrayed internal rhetoric previously, becomes the springboard for his discussion of the most pervasive of social phenomena.

Burke argues that socialization is rhetorical because it is concerned with identification between the individual and society: "The individual person, striving to form himself in accordance with the communicative norms that match the cooperative ways of his society, is by the same token concerned with the rhetoric of identification" (*Rhetoric* 39). That is, a person is constantly exposed to patterns of communication that, by their very pervasiveness, express or create social mores and ethical imperatives. She can either mold her behavior to fit those norms or, as Burke has suggested earlier, rationalize behavior that does not quite meet the external standard.

What is significant about how Burke explains socialization is that it is not rhetorical because the individual is a passive audience for societal pressure for identification, but because the individual uses internal rhetoric to create identification with social mores:

> To act upon himself persuasively, he must variously resort to images and ideas that are formative. Education ("indoctrination") exerts such pressure upon him from without; he completes the process from

> within. If he does not somehow act to tell himself (as his own audience) what the various brands of rhetoricians have told him, his persuasion is not complete. (*Rhetoric* 39)

It is difficult to reconcile this description, in which individuals appear to control their own socialization, with Burke's other discussions of how much the individual is created and controlled by language. In his earlier work, *Permanence and Change,* Burke argues that "our minds, as linguistic products, are composed of concepts (verbally molded) which select certain relationships as meaningful" (35). After the *Rhetoric of Motives,* Burke makes an even stronger statement about the linguistic construction of human reality and personality:

> Do we simply use words, or do they not also use us? An "ideology" is like a god coming down to earth, where it will inhabit a place pervaded by its presence. An "ideology" is like a spirit taking up its abode in a body: it makes that body hop around in certain ways; and that same body would have hopped around in different ways had a different ideology happened to inhabit it. ("Definition of Man" 6)

An argument could be made that the description of socialization as purposive internal rhetoric is not fallaciously rationalistic because it relies on Burke's recognition of unconscious identification or, implicitly, on Mead's description of internalized social voices to account for the "voice[s] within." Support for this view might be found in "Rhetoric and Poetics," where Burke describes socialization as a "spontaneous" identification with "family, nation, . . . and so on" (301). That explanation would still have to account for the emphasis on action in this passage, since Burke consistently associates conscious purpose with human "action" (as opposed to mechanistic "motion"; see *A Grammar of Motives* 14).

Internal and external rhetorics intersect, then, as a person receives and absorbs public discourse. The individual is an audience for the rhetorical identifications of public discourse insofar as she is exposed to it, but actually completes the identification by becoming her own audience. Just as Burke used Freud earlier to complicate the relationship between the internal rhetors and the various audiences with whom those rhetors must identify, he again elaborates the model of internal rhetoric by introducing internalized (and external) social voices. In this audience-centered perspective on internal rhetoric, the rhetors become multiple and overdetermined. The internal audience attends to both the internal rhetors and "the various brands of [external] rhetoricians" in identifying with societal norms. This final observation on the power of internal rhetoric makes us realize that Burke has demonstrated that the "range of rhetoric" is pervasive not only in the human world but also in the construction of the interior psychological world of the individual.

Throughout his discussion of internal rhetoric, Burke compares internal and external rhetoric, but in this last section of his argument he suggests that internal rhetoric is necessary for the completion, the efficacy, of the public rhetorics for which the subject is an audience. In this formulation, he broadens the model of internal rhetoric from a preliminary or alternative to public rhetoric—that is, as an inventional aid, as for Shaftesbury, or a practice of ethical deliberation, as for Whately—to a necessary condition for the fulfillment of public rhetoric. He sees this complementary act as essential for all varieties of persuasive discourse, from the pervasive rhetoricality that results in socialization to the pointed rhetoric of teachers and other public rhetors. Internal rhetoric is thus a fundamental concept for Burke's system of rhetoric and a core characteristic of human beings as "the symbol-using (symbol-making, symbol-misusing) animal" ("Definition of Man," 16).

Burke's discussion of internal rhetoric, then, is pivotal between his two "main aspects of rhetoric: its use of *identification* and its nature as *addressed*" (*Rhetoric* 45), as well as in his overall project of establishing the inseparability of language use from human nature and reality. He emphasizes the impact of language on human lives in the "Definition of Man":

> The "symbol-using animal," yes, obviously. But can we bring ourselves to realize just what that formula implies, how overwhelmingly much of what we mean by "reality" has been built up for us through nothing but our symbol systems? . . . What is our "reality" for today (beyond the paper-thin line of our own particular lives) but all this clutter of symbols about the past combined with whatever things we know mainly through maps, magazines, newspapers, and the like about the present? (5)

Burke thus presents a radically epistemic view of symbolic action in the world. Not only is our knowledge of external reality constructed by language, but so is our knowledge of the reality inside of us:

> In being a link between us and the nonverbal, words are by the same token a screen separating us from the nonverbal—though the statement gets tangled in its own traces, since so much of the "we" that is separated from the nonverbal by the verbal would not even exist were it not for the verbal. (5)

Burke's definition of humans as symbol-using animals, then, means that "symbolicity" affects the very nature of human identity. Burke has taken the problem that has bedeviled rhetoricians and anti-rhetoricians alike for centuries—the relationship between words and things—and shown how it plays out within the human being. If language is the means by which we create not only our worldview but also ourselves, and if rhetoric is "an essential function of language itself" (*Rhetoric* 43)—"Wherever there is persuasion, there is rhetoric. And wherever there is 'meaning,' there is 'persuasion'" (*Rhetoric* 172)—then Burke presents a thoroughly rhetorical view of the way we have created our worlds and our own identities.

In my study of the two dominant twentieth-century rhetorical theories, then, I have demonstrated a remarkable revolution in the history of internal rhetoric. Kenneth Burke and Perelman and Olbrechts-Tyteca use depth psychology, with its explanations of and focus on the unconscious, to transform the concept of internal rhetoric from a concern with specific faculties and ethical imperatives—exemplified most thoroughly in the previous chapter—to a more holistic, pervasive phenomenon. Given Perelman and Olbrechts-Tyteca's citation and Burke's evocation of Isocrates, I might argue that the philosophers discussed in chapter 2 play out the Platonic-Aristotelean model of internal rhetoric, while those in this chapter develop an elaboration of Isocrates' epistemic model.

Similar to Isocrates' expansive claims for the role of *logos* in society, Burke and Perelman and Olbrechts-Tyteca open the realm of internal and external rhetoric to all aspects of human life. Burke does so by focusing on how language creates identification and division among and within people, defining rhetoric as *"an essential function of language itself . . . the use of language as a symbolic means of inducing cooperation in beings that by nature respond to symbols"* (*Rhetoric* 43). *Iden-*

tification, rather than *persuasion,* is Burke's key term for rhetoric: the former emphasizing the cooperative aspect of rhetoric while the latter "implies the presence or threat of an adversary" and thus carries an "'agonistic' or competitive stress" (*Rhetoric* 52). Rhetoric is necessary even within the psyche for the coordination of inner cooperation, his counterexample being the neurotic person: "Considered rhetorically, the victim of a neurotic conflict is torn by parliamentary wrangling. . . . Rhetorically, the neurotic's every attempt to legislate for his own conduct is disorganized by rival factions within his own dissociated self" (*Rhetoric* 23). Moreover, Burke argues that our selves are created and mediated through language; so internal rhetoric becomes of crucial importance as a filter, an ongoing terministic screen, for the public discourses we are constantly exposed to.

Perelman and Olbrechts-Tyteca also greatly enlarge the realm of rhetoric by examining how people agree and disagree on everything within their experience: "Instead of basing our philosophy on definitive, unquestionable truths, our starting point is that men and groups of men adhere to opinions of all sorts with a variable intensity, which we can only know by putting it to the test" (511). Just as Burke's key term for rhetoric is identification, Perelman and Olbrechts-Tyteca's must be adherence: "the mind's adherence to the theses presented for its assent" (4). They thus see such phenomena as facts, truths, values, and presumptions through the lens of audience agreement: something is considered a fact, for example, if (and as long as) a "community of minds" agrees that it is a fact. Perelman and Olbrechts-Tyteca also expand rhetoric into the psychic realm, arguing against the logical view of self-deliberation. They classify self-deliberation as argumentative (or rhetorical) because it is impossible to categorize deliberation as purely rational and because different internalized audiences generate differing rationalizations (or, as Burke would have them, motivations) for the same decision or act.

Burke and Perelman and Olbrechts-Tyteca share references to the unconscious workings of the mind that premise much of twentieth-century psychology. Previous accounts of internal rhetoric have outlined an ideal: conscious, motivationally pure discursive action on one part of the psyche by another. When such internal discourse is not consciously controlled, it is illegitimate, seen to have a "pernicious" effect. Burke recognizes the possibility of deceptive internal rhetoric, but does not equate it purely with unconscious rhetorical motives.[22] Rather, he sees rhetorical motives as being overdetermined, never purely conscious and with unconscious motives never the only "real" ones. In recognizing the rhetorical relations among mostly undefined factions in the psyche and between individual and societal discourses, Burke sees internal rhetoric as a definitive human trait.

Perelman and Olbrechts-Tyteca use an awareness of the unconscious to argue against the logicians' traditional view of deliberation as being purely logical or reasonable, an instance of address to a hypothetical universal audience. They claim, instead, that persons can never be certain of the reasonableness of their inner deliberation, since irrational motives may be adhered to unconsciously. At the same time, Perelman and Olbrechts-Tyteca, as well as Burke, criticize depth psychology for the narrow absolutism of its view of rationalization. Perelman and Olbrechts-Tyteca critique psychoanalytical rationalization for its acontextual clinging to a single "real" motive in the face of the various internal and potential audiences for which "rationalizations" are legitimate reasonings. Burke argues that the psychologists' view of rationalization is an imperialism of terms, a critique of motives in terms that the individual involved may never have been exposed to. In each case, the rhetoricians use depth psychology for the radically disruptive effects of the unconscious but reject its more conservative reality claims.

Finally, I should note that Burke and Perelman and Olbrechts-Tyteca radically expand the function of internal rhetoric by restoring, à la Isocrates, its epistemic (in addition to its ethical) activities in the human psyche. Burke argues that both our external and psychic worlds are created and known through language use. Internal rhetoric serves as the nexus between these internal and external symbolic worlds. For Perelman and Olbrechts-Tyteca, the dichotomy between the epistemic concern with knowledge and the ethical concern with pragmatic action is a false one, born of a false separation of faculties within the human psyche. Facts, truths, presumptions, and values are all premises for argumentation that claim various degrees of adherence by their audiences. Internal rhetoric is thus a way of knowing the world and our own minds as well as a way of deciding on or persuading to action.

I have come to the end of a series of historical sketches of how certain mental processes have been related to public rhetoric, a phenomenon I have called internal rhetoric. In the following chapter, I supplement these rhetorical perspectives with a rhetorical reading of certain psychological frameworks, which make explicit the role of language—and, I argue, internal rhetoric—in constructing what we experience as our "selves." My model of internal rhetoric thus expands from being an activity characteristic of the psyche to being an activity constitutive of the psyche—a conceptualization that not only reiterates and emphasizes the socialized nature of internal rhetoric but also touches on its role in individual and generic human development.

4

The Construction of Selves by Internal Rhetoric

> They continued to walk onward, while the elder traveller exhorted his companion to make good speed and persevere in the path, discoursing so aptly that his arguments seemed rather to spring up in the bosom of his auditor than to be suggested by himself.
>
> —Nathaniel Hawthorne, "Young Goodman Brown"

Thus far, I have discussed internal rhetoric mostly in terms of individual acts of self-persuasion or self-clarification, done "in varying degrees of deliberateness and unawareness" (Burke, *Rhetoric of Motives* 35), from the reasonable process of ethical decision making to the emotional pleadings of the lustful dark horse. Kenneth Burke has suggested how significant are these individual acts over time, as they accumulate into a person's socialization. It is this cumulative effect of rhetorical self-construction that occupies the present chapter, for which I temporarily leave my rhetorical and philosophical sources for psychological ones. In doing so, I follow Burke's lead in looking at psychology from a rhetorical perspective.[1] I here argue that psychologies focusing on the role language plays in shaping the mind are, in an important sense, rhetorical; that is, the adaptive function they describe language performing vis-à-vis the mind is necessarily a rhetorical function. Instead of a "dialogical self" (Hermans and Kempen), a "semiotic self" (Wiley), or the "literary mind" (Turner), I here posit a "rhetorical self."[2]

The rhetorical self goes beyond the aspects of internal rhetoric I have derived from various philosophers and rhetoricians; rather, to argue that our very selves are rhetorically constructed means that we are shaped by rhetorical language uses (internal and external) long before we are aware of conducting rational or emotional debates within ourselves. While other theorists, notably Lacan,[3] have posited the linguistic structure of the mind, few have explored the continuity of this structure with explicit rhetorical acts such as public oratory. In the conclusion I discuss in more detail my own multilayered view of the rhetorical self, which I prepare for in this chapter by explicating the rhetorical nature of George Herbert Mead's and Lev Vygotsky's social psychologies.

Mead and Vygotsky's theories of the social formation of the mind make explicit what has been implicit in many of the theorists I have discussed so far: that is, the internalization of social language. Mead explains how consciousness evolves from animals to humans through the internalization of increasingly complex social gestures and language. In doing so, he accounts for the normative or rhetorical force of internalized social voices. Next, I argue that Vygotsky's theory of the social development of language and thought complements Mead's evolutionary scheme. While Vygotsky emphasizes the cognitive role of language internalization, the characteristics he attributes to adult inner speech reveal its rhetorical origins and functions. Similarly, the roles that the "I" and "me" take in Mead's theory of the mind and self reveal the extent to which the rhetorical pressures that Burke characterizes as "socialization" are internalized, actively working to continuously shape and reshape a person's sense of self. Together, Mead and Vygotsky provide a comprehensive view of the role that social language use plays in the rhetorical construction of an individual's thought processes, consciousness, and mind.

Evolution and Development of the Rhetorical Self

It is difficult to make any claims about the origins and evolution of language, given the lack of prehistoric data or extant species exhibiting early evolutionary stages of "true" language,[4] and also given the plethora of imaginative speculations about the origins of language like the "bow-wow" theory or the "pooh-pooh" theory.[5] The search for the evolution of rhetorical behavior need not adhere to stringent biological standards, however: rather than looking for such determinants as specific sites in the brain where rhetoric originates, we can look for behavioral practices in which social animals—including humans—attempt to influence others, and see how those rhetorical behaviors become internalized in humans to create rhetorical selves.

The first impulse toward rhetorical behavior is found in the instinctive gestures of animals as well as humans: thus, in *Comparative Rhetoric,* George Kennedy spends his first chapter on "Rhetoric among Social Animals." Kennedy offers a broad, even interspecial definition of rhetoric in this context:

> I shall argue in this book that rhetoric, in essence, is a form of mental and emotional energy. . . . The emotional reaction in the mind of the individual, consciously or unconsciously, then sparks utterance—speech or gesture—aimed at affecting the situation. Utterance requires physical energy and conveys rhetorical energy; so do gestures.[6] (4)

Instinctive gestures are a form of communication eliciting a response and thus have a rhetorical component. But the rhetoricity at this level of gesture may remind us of George Campbell's epigram that "the first impulse towards the attainment of every art is Nature" (lxxiv).

George Herbert Mead looks at gestures not only as a precursor to linguistic communication but as the first step in the evolution of the conscious mind—and, for my purposes, the rhetorical self. Going beyond Charles Darwin's assertion that gestures express individual mental and emotional states,[7] Mead follows Wilhelm Wundt in considering the gesture originally a social rather than an expressive act:

> Within any given social act, an adjustment is effected, by means of gestures, of the actions of one organism involved to the actions of another; the gestures are movements of the first organism which act as specific stimuli calling forth the (socially) appropriate responses of the second organism. (Mead 14n. 9)

Gestures are social acts in that they call forth a response of some sort from other participants in the social setting. Mead's use of the biological term *organism* reflects his argument that animals as well as humans use gestures to converse (14), using as his example the posturing of dogs preceding (or averting) a fight. At the level of pure gesture, these exchanges do not involve forethought; rather, they operate on an instinctive, nonlinguistic level.[8]

The next step in the evolutionary ladder to language, mind, and what we usually think of as rhetoric is the significant gesture. At this level, intention becomes a factor; a significant gesture is more explicitly rhetorical than an instinctive one because it is intended to evoke a particular response in another individual. Gestures become significant, according to Mead, when they have meaning for the individual performing them. Such meaning comes when an individual internalizes the possible responses to the gesture:

> Gestures become significant symbols when they implicitly arouse in an individual making them the same response which they explicitly arouse, or are supposed to arouse, in other individuals, the individuals to whom they are addressed; and in all conversations of gestures within the social process, . . . the individual's consciousness of the content and flow of meaning involved depends on his thus taking the attitude of the other toward his own gestures. (47)

In this case, the meaning of the gesture for the agent (and for the community) is the anticipated response it calls forth from the other participants in the social act. On a nonlinguistic level, an example of a significant gesture might be how people wave their hands upon meeting with or parting from friends.

Language is a particular case of significant gesturing; for Mead, it is "a symbol which answers to a meaning in the experience of the first individual [the gesturing agent] and which calls out that meaning in the second individual [the recipient]" (46).[9] He argues that language develops from instinctive vocal gestures because vocal gestures, being heard by the agent in the same way as by the recipient, have particular power to reflexively call forth the same response in the agent as in the recipient (160–61). This progression, from instinctive to significant gestures and from vocal gestures to language, provides an entire genealogy of hortatory, and therefore rhetorical, human action.

Thus, rhetoric is not a specific application of language use. It evolves simultaneously with language out of the same patterns of social gesturing. All language is imbued with—but not exhausted by—rhetorical function.

This view of language and rhetoric as evolving from significant gestures provides the basis for Mead's claim that the mind develops out of these social acts of gesturing. Just as gestures and language are originally rhetorical—intended to influence other people in specific ways[10]—thought, too, is rhetorical, calling forth attitudes or actions in the self according to the anticipated responses of others. According to Mead, people's conscious minds evolve out of the linguistic, social interactions they have engaged in:

> Only in terms of gestures as significant symbols is the existence of mind or intelligence possible; for only in terms of gestures which are significant symbols can thinking—which is simply an internalized or implicit conversation of the individual with himself by means of gestures—take place. (47)

Thinking, then, is an internalized "conversation of gestures," patterned after the social communication that the individual has experienced with others.[11] Thought develops not merely from internalized stimulus and response but from the ability to anticipate the response of others and to control one's future actions or attitudes accordingly: "In order that thought may exist there must be symbols, vocal gestures generally, which arouse in the individual himself the response which he is calling out in the other, and such that from the point of view of that response he is able to direct his later conduct" (73). For Mead, it is this ability to project into the future—"the future as present in terms of ideas" (119)—that characterizes the conscious mind, distinguishing human "reflective intelligence" from animal intelligence.

The last step toward the evolution of the mind (and what I argue is the rhetorical self) is the ability of the individual to anticipate not only the responses of other individuals but also the expectations of the communities of which they are members. Mead writes, "The organized community or social group which gives to the individual his unity of self may be called 'the generalized other.' The attitude of the generalized other is the attitude of the whole community" (154). The "whole community," for Mead, is not a monolithic social entity, nor is a person's "unity of self" a monolithic self. His first example illustrates the particularity and therefore multiplicity of the generalized other: "In the case of such a social group as a ball team, the team is the generalized other in so far as it enters—as an organized social process or social activity—into the experience of any one of the individual members of it" (154). Because generalized others are various and situational, when Mead writes of the "unity of self" (154) or of the "complete self" (155), he is arguing not that the mind is an undifferentiated integer but that it comprehends the many organized social processes that it internalizes. The generalized other, then, is Mead's shorthand for representing how people incorporate socially structured sets of attitudes into a complex, capable-of-being-conscious self. In the second section of this chapter I will argue that the generalized other provides the key to my reading of Mead's self as a rhetorical one.

Mead thus provides us with an evolutionary—behavioral, rather than biological—perspective on language and rhetoric that explains how people internalize social behaviors, creating the conscious mind. To get from evolution to individual development requires only a minor metaphorical leap: as I learned in undergraduate biology, "ontogeny recapitulates phylogeny."[12] It should be no surprise, then, that Lev Vygotsky's schema of the intertwining developments of language and intellect in children echoes, in many ways, Mead's sketch of the evolution of language, especially since they both start with Wundt's discussion of gestures.

Up to this point, this study of internal rhetoric has implicitly been analyzing the extent to which *adult* thought processes have been perceived to be, or might be described as being, rhetorical. This bias is an extension of the historical thrust of rhetoric as a prescriptive pedagogical discipline. Its goal has not typically been to describe rhetorical strategies used by people at various stages of their lives but to teach or analyze the art of discourse and its uses in public (adult) settings. A related discipline, composition theory, has departed from this exclusive focus on adults, with groundbreaking studies like James Britton et al.'s *Development of Writing Abilities,* 11–18 and James Moffett's *Teaching the Universe of Discourse* initiating a whole field of research on the development of writing ability.[13] The broader study of language development in linguistics and psychology has had a much longer history, some of which is reflected in this discussion of Vygotsky. My analysis of Vygotsky from a rhetorical perspective thus offers a rapprochement between rhetorical theory and studies of language development in other disciplines.

A significant preliminary finding of Vygotsky's research is that thought and speech do not develop in a static relation to one another: "The most important fact uncovered through the genetic study of thought and speech is that their relation undergoes many changes. Progress in thought and progress in speech are not parallel. Their two growth curves cross and recross" (*Thought and Language* 68). Thus, the four stages in which Vygotsky sees language developing are often marked by their relationship to the intellectual development going on at the same time. The intertwining developments of speech and thought will become particularly significant in the second section of this chapter, when I use Vygotsky's characterizations of inner speech to describe the cognitive aspects of internal rhetoric.

Vygotsky's first stage of language development, the "primitive or natural stage" (86), corresponds to preintellectual speech, in which a child's noises provide emotional release and social contact without being connected to intellectual development (81). During this stage, the child learns to make gestures to communicate with others. Vygotsky uses the example of how a child's grasping for an out-of-reach object becomes a social rather than an object-oriented behavior:

> When the mother comes to the child's aid and realizes his movement indicates something, the situation changes fundamentally. Pointing becomes a gesture for others. The child's unsuccessful attempt engenders a reaction not from the object he seeks but *from another person*. . . . At this juncture there occurs a change in that movement's function: from an object-oriented movement it becomes a movement aimed at another person, a means of establishing relations. (*Mind in Society* 56; emphasis Vygotsky's)

Vygotsky notes that this behavior on the child's part becomes a gesture for others before the child consciously intends it as a social gesture: "Every function in the child's cultural development appears twice: first, on the social level, and later, on the individual level; first, *between* people *(interpsychological),* and then *inside* the child *(intrapsychological)*" (*Mind in Society* 57; emphasis Vygotsky's). Like Wundt (and Mead, evolutionarily), Vygotsky argues that these pointing gestures are "the first stage in the development of human speech" (*Thought and Language* 72).[14] Vygotsky therefore sees the earliest manifestations of language use in children as social, arguing that "the primary function of speech, both in children and adults, is communication, social contact" (34). His example of the child pointing leads me to make the further assertion that even at this earliest stage of language development in the child, one primary function is rhetorical—gestures done to influence the behavior of others.

Vygotsky says little of the second stage, which is also less relevant to an ontogeny of internal rhetoric: "It is manifested by the correct use of grammatical forms and structures before the child has understood the logical operations for which they stand. . . . He masters syntax of speech before syntax of thought" (87).

The third stage, however, marks a significant moving inward of rhetorical intent. During this stage of language development, the functions of language begin to differentiate between communicative and egocentric speech, both of which are still manifested externally. Egocentric speech differs from communicative speech in its personal nature:

> Speech is interiorized psychologically before it is interiorized physically. Egocentric speech is inner speech in its functions; it is speech on its way inward, intimately tied up with the ordering of the child's behavior, already partly incomprehensible to others, yet still overt in form. (86)

In the same way that the child has already learned to influence the behavior of others by social speech and gestures, during this third stage the child begins to influence its own behavior linguistically—or, more to the point of this argument, rhetorically.

At this ur-stage of internal rhetoric, children do not yet differentiate themselves as an audience separate from other people in the room. Vygotsky shows experimentally that children have "the illusion of being understood" in their egocentric speech:

> They believe that their thoughts, even those that are poorly expressed or unarticulated, belong to all participants. This, according to Grünbaum, points to the insufficient separation of the child's individual psyche from the social whole. (232)

That is, the child begins to use language for personal functions, but perceives such speech as social in the same way that the communicative speech it grows out of is social. In a sense, then, children are exhorting themselves much as they exhort others in their communicative speech acts.

Further explanation of the "personal functions" of egocentric speech is in order because it is not exhausted by its exhortative, rhetorical function. Rather, Vygotsky characterizes egocentric speech by its cognitive functions. He demonstrates that egocentric speech is used by children in problem-solving activities; that is, it tends to erupt when researchers introduce "frustrations and difficulties" (29) into a play situation. When children encounter obstructions in their activities, they switch from fairly automatic behavior patterns to a sudden awareness of their activity, and this awareness is expressed in egocentric speech. The third stage, then, is "distinguished by external signs, external operations that are used as aids in the solution of internal problems" (87). This is the stage when the courses of intellectual and language development coincide and reinforce each other as children develop the use of egocentric speech for intellectual purposes. Functionally, egocentric speech develops from being "a means of expression and release of tension" to becoming "an instrument of thought in the proper sense—in seeking and planning the solution of a problem" (31).[15] Because of this intermeshing of speech and thought during the third and fourth stages of language development, the development process itself changes. I will briefly sketch the fourth stage before describing the significance that Vygotsky attributes to the altered process.

The last stage of language development that Vygotsky traces is the "ingrowth" stage, the stage in which internal rhetoric fully develops. This fourth stage is when children begin to use "inner, soundless speech" (87) to accomplish reasoning and problem-solving tasks that in the third stage evoked egocentric speech: "The external operation turns inward and undergoes a profound change in the process" (87). Vygotsky observes, as part of his study of the apparent disappearance of egocentric speech, that school-aged children perform mentally the same kind of problem solving that younger children do verbally in egocentric speech:

> Our observation that at the age when this change [when egocentric speech "goes underground"] is taking place children facing difficult situations resort now to egocentric speech, now to silent reflection, indicates that the two can be functionally equivalent. (33)

The value of observing egocentric speech, then, is the window it provides on inner speech: Vygotsky posits this as "an excellent method for studying inner speech 'live,' as it were, while its structural and functional peculiarities are being shaped" (86). While Vygotsky treats egocentric and inner speech as primarily cognitive in function, the rhetorical effect of such speech is shown in how problem solving affects the child's immediate behavior. I will return to the rhetorical aspects of inner speech in the next section, but first I want to note the significant change Vygotsky attributes to the process of language development during its third and fourth stages.

In the earliest stages of both linguistic and intellectual development, Vygotsky notes parallels between apes and humans: "Anthropoids display an intellect somewhat like man's *in certain respects* (the embryonic use of tools) and a language somewhat like man's *in totally different respects* (the phonetic aspect of their speech, its release function, the beginnings of a social function)" (79–80; Vygotsky's emphasis). Such parallels indicate that development processes are biologically determined in these earliest, separate stages of linguistic and intellectual development. Later, once the two developing capabilities merge, language becomes a tool of thought and thus aids in the development of thought along lines that are determined by language's social nature. The latter stages of linguistic and intellectual development are thus qualitatively different from the earlier stages:

> *The nature of the development itself changes,* from biological to sociohistorical. Verbal thought is not an innate, natural form of behavior, but is determined by a historical-cultural process and has specific properties and laws that cannot be found in the natural forms of thought and speech. (94; Vygotsky's emphasis)

The social nature of language means that social context shapes the intellectual development fostered by language—that which Vygotsky characterizes as the "higher forms of behavior" and defines as "the invention and use of signs as auxiliary means of solving a given psychological problem" (*Mind in Society* 52). Because verbal thought is sociohistorically shaped, Vygotsky argues that psychologists cannot make assertions about "the timelessly childish," but must instead try "to discover the 'historically childish'" (*Thought and Language* 57).[16] Vygotsky predicts that different proportions of egocentric and communicative speech will be observed in different social settings among different ages of children (56). The significance of this sociohistorical shaping of intellect is not limited to childhood, however: Mary Belenky and her coauthors cite Vygotsky with respect to the differential development processes women undergo in social situations that limit their linguistic development (32–33).

Moreover, the sociohistorical nature of linguistic and intellectual development is significant for this study of internal rhetoric because it changes the nature of the posited internal rhetorical agents. Before Mead and Vygotsky, these agents were portrayed as innate, ahistorical parts of the psyche: *phrena/thumos,* reason/emotions/will, or superego/ego/id.[17] Both Mead and Vygotsky see the development of certain aspects of the psyche as conditioned by personal, social, and historical circumstance, so their contribution to a theory of internal rhetoric is a much more flexible notion of internal rhetorical agency than that of the earlier models.

A Sociohistorical Version of the Rhetorical Self

Mead's discussion of how the mind evolves and Vygotsky's sketch of how inner speech develops suggest that language is internalized not just as grammar, syntax, and object reference but also as hortatory imperatives for thought and behavior. The two models explain both how internal rhetoric originates and how internal and external rhetorics accumulate to shape rhetorical selves—an accumulation that does not stop at puberty or maturity, but continues throughout life.[18] How, then, does mature internal rhetoric and its ongoing accumulation, the rhetorical self, look from a Meadian/Vygotskian perspective, insofar as I can make generalizations about concepts that are both sociohistorically constrained and in constant process?

Although I have just argued that Mead and Vygotsky give us models of people internalizing the persuasive function of language, both characterize their portrayals of the mind as cognitive. They are not opposing cognition to rhetoric, however, as Isocrates implicitly does when he insists that *logos* is a synthesis of persuasion and clarification and as Plato explicitly does when he opposes rhetoric to philosophy. Mead does not call his Self cognitive in opposition to persuasive, but rather to distinguish it from affective theories of the self:

> Self-consciousness, rather than affective experience with its motor accompaniments, provides the core and primary structure of the self, which is thus essentially a cognitive rather than an emotional phenomenon. . . . The essence of the self . . . lies in the internalized conversation of gestures which constitutes thinking, or in terms of which thought and reflection proceeds. (173)

Mead's "cognitive" self lies on the persuasive, hortative end of Isocrates' spectrum of the functions of *logos*. Vygotsky's description of inner speech does recall the cognitive, clarifying function of Isocratean *logos,* but Vygotskian inner speech reveals its rhetorical character in its function and characteristics.[19]

Vygotsky's discussion of inner speech focuses more on the internal use of language to articulate ideas than its use in communicating or persuading, the premise of the conversational models of internal rhetoric we have seen so far. Yet such verbal thought does have a deliberative, rhetorical function, because problem solving affects future behavior. Vygotsky's description of inner speech is very similar to the way that Achilleus uses internal rhetoric to clarify a confusing situation and determine a course of action (chapter 1). What Vygotsky adds to this picture of inner speech or internal rhetoric is the sociohistorical situatedness of such reasoning: Deliberation or problem solving is not a timeless, innate procedure but is structured by the social and linguistic/rhetorical experiences of the deliberator.

Even the syntax that Vygotsky attributes to inner speech reveals its social origin and rhetorical nature insofar as it is addressed to a particular, intimate audience.[20] Vygotsky distinguishes between high-context speech situations, in which the interlocutors know each other well and can leave many things unspoken, and low-context speech situations, in which the interlocutors may be absent (writing) or alien to one another and everything needs to be made explicit. Inner speech is the ultimate high-context speech situation, and thus it has an abbreviated syntax and is commonly perceived to be "disconnected and incomplete" compared with external speech (235). According to Vygotsky's analysis, what gets truncated in inner speech is the subject, so that it consists of almost "pure predication" (236).[21] Degrees of similar truncation of the subject can be seen in external speech among intimates or in answer to a question, the determining factor being the amount of social or conversational context or prior knowledge for a given speech act.[22] The extreme of highest contextualization is inner speech, because a person is talking to herself: "We know what we are thinking about; i.e., we always know the subject and the situation. And since the subject of our inner dialogue is already known, we may just imply it" (243). Since Vygotsky sees inner speech as situationally grounded (as well as sociohistorically determined), the subject is always present nonlinguistically. What this syntactic peculiarity demonstrates is that even mature inner speech is implicitly addressed, one of Kenneth Burke's two definitive characteristics of rhetoric.

While Vygotsky's inner speech shows traces of its social and rhetorical origins, Mead fully supports the conversational models of internal rhetoric by dividing the self into the "I" and the "me," mental components conducting the internal communication that Mead identifies as thought.[23] Briefly, Mead distinguishes two facets or "phases" of the mind: "The 'I' is the response of the organism to the attitudes of others; the 'me' is the organized set of attitudes of others which one himself assumes" (175). Through the lens of internal rhetoric, the "I" and the "me" are rhetorical agents just as surely as the emotions and reason were for Bacon and Shaftesbury, but they are constituted differently from the agents in faculty psychology.

Rather than describing the mind as composed of innate faculties, Mead uses the "me" to denote internalized social structures (what today might be called ideologies): "The 'me' represent[s] that group of attitudes which stands for others in the community, especially that organized group of responses which we have detailed in discussing the game on the one hand and social institutions on the other" (194).[24] The "me" is thus our internal representation of socially determined attitudes; it is, to some extent, the normative voice of the community that Freud associates with the superego.[25] Since the "me" is constituted according to the structures of society present to the individual, Mead's method of analyzing the mind—and internal rhetoric—is historically and culturally situated; it does not depend on the universalized faculties we have seen in earlier psychologies.

Functionally, the "me" makes a person self-conscious, as opposed to merely conscious:

> And it is due to the individual's ability to take the attitudes of these others in so far as they can be organized that he gets self-consciousness. The taking of all of those organized sets of attitudes gives him his "me"; that is the self he is aware of. (175)

Because a person has internalized the attitudes of others in the "me," she can perceive herself as an "other" or object and thus be self-conscious—that is, conscious of the self in the same way she might be conscious of her environs and other people. The "me" is, in fact, perceived by Mead as creating an environment for the activity of the "I": the "me" "presents the situation within which conduct takes place" (277). By internalizing a social context for the actions of the self as agent, the "me" provides a frame of reference for consciousness of the self.

The "I" always acts in the context of the "me," Mead argues, reacting or responding to it: "The 'I' is his action over against that social situation within his own conduct" (175). Mead presents the "I" in two contexts: as a "phase" of the self that is more or less the obverse of the "me," and as the "biological individual." In the first sense, Mead emphasizes that we are not aware of the "I" in the same way we are aware of the "me." The "I" is always our present, agential self, which becomes a "me" as the moment passes and we remember our past actions in social context: "The 'I' of this moment is present in the 'me' of the next moment. There again I cannot turn around quick enough to catch myself. I become a 'me' in so far as I remember what I said" (174). Thus, although the "I" always acts in the context of and responds to the socialized "me," its actions are not determined by the "me": "It is because of the 'I' that we say we are never fully aware of what we are, that we surprise ourselves by our own action" (174). Mead emphasizes the element of unpredictability of the "I": "I want to call attention particularly to the fact that this response of the 'I' is something that is more or less uncertain" (176). He recognizes that we may have different "me"s, internalized social attitudes, conflicting with one another at any given time, so the "I" may respond to any or none of them. This lack of determinism in human conduct is important: "The 'I' gives the sense of freedom, of initiative" (177). The "I" thus comprises the creative aspects of the personality, "the immediate attitude of the artist, the inventor, the scientist in his discovery, in general in the action of the 'I' which cannot be calculated and which involves a reconstruction of society" (214). For Mead, then, the "I" is the self as agent over against the "me," which is the self as socially constructed individual.

The second context in which Mead discusses the "I" is as a "biological individual," which he portrays as the primal part of the human self. He relates the biological "I" and the social "me" in a brief developmental sketch that resonates with Vygotsky's more complex analysis discussed earlier:

> It is necessary to emphasize the wide stretch between the direct immediate life of the child [the "I"] and this self growing in his conduct [the "me"]. The latter is almost imposed from without. He may passively accept the individual that the group about him assigns to him as himself. This is very different from the passionate asser-

> tive biological individual, that loves and hates and embraces and strikes. *He* is never an object; *his* is a life of direct suffering and action. (370)

In the sense that it is both developmentally early and passionate, Mead's biological individual "I" is an expression of Freud's id and more recent portrayals of the functions of the human amygdala.[26] It also recalls various faculty psychology accounts that make the emotions more primitive than reason.[27] Mead also stresses the unreflectiveness of the biological self, as he does that of the "I": "It is this [biological] individual in action, with his attention on the object. He does not come into the field of his own vision" (372). The main difference between the biological "I" and the "I" as it is described in contrast to the "me" is that the biological "I" is biologically determined, made up of "primitive human impulses" (349).

Mead's description of the "I" is thus complex: conforming to biological imperatives, responding to the influences of various "me"s, but at the same time unpredictable and creative as an agent. At the extreme, Mead argues that the "I" can change society by its actions:

> Great figures in history bring about very fundamental changes. These profound changes which take place through the action of individual minds are only the extreme expression of the sort of changes that take place steadily through reactions which are not simply those of a "me" but of an "I." (202)

So even though the individual must act within social contexts and has actually internalized those constructs, the fact that the "I" can respond variously to social stimuli means that it is a force for social change.

However, Mead never isolates this ability to change society from the pervasive social contexts in which it must act:

> The only way in which I can react against the disapproval of the entire community is by setting up a higher sort of community which in a certain sense out-votes the one we find. A person may reach a point of going against the whole world about him; he may stand out by himself over against it. But to do that he has to speak with the voice of reason to himself. He has to comprehend the voices of the past and of the future. That is the only way in which the self can get a voice which is more than the voice of the community. (167–68)

The individual always acts in response to a community, but that does not mean that her response is predetermined: "We must not forget this other capacity, that of replying to the community and insisting on the gesture of the community changing" (168). The individual, as described by Mead, is constrained by society but not determined by it because the individual typically has many communities to which she can respond—society is never monolithic or, perhaps more to the point, monovocal. The same self-consciousness that is generated by internalizing communal organization can question and choose among communities.

The observation that Mead considers the "I" to be the agential self does not mean that the "me" has no agency whatsoever in the psyche. The role of the "me" in internal rhetoric is complex because of the normative pressures it exerts on the "I." The "me" may be an audience for the "I," but it is a participatory audience, one that has the power to judge and respond to the actions of the "I":

> He becomes not only self-conscious but also self-critical; and thus, through self-criticism, social control over individual behavior or conduct operates by virtue of the social origin and basis of such criticism. That is to say, self-criticism is essentially social criticism, and behavior controlled by self-criticism is essentially behavior controlled socially. (255)

This characterization of how the "me" controls behavior complicates any simplistic "rhetor (or 'I') as agent/audience (or 'me') as patient" dichotomy in a Meadian view of internal rhetoric.

Mead, then, leaves us with a rhetorical self based on the social evolution of the mind, consciousness, and self-consciousness that still leaves room for individual impulse, creativity, and choice. The socially constructed "me" and the unpredictable "I" are not specific faculties within the mind, nor do they exist in a fixed ratio in any single personality or over a population. Rather, they are situationally functional and situationally related, so that in between the extremes of mob action (mostly social control) and the expression of genius (mostly individual control) lies the vast majority of human social life, with its variously conventional and individualistic opportunities and situations.

This chapter—indeed, the whole of part two—has taken us a quantum leap from my earlier snapshots of internal rhetoric as conscious acts of deliberation ideally controlled by an individual. In chapter 3, I used Burke and Perelman and Olbrechts-Tyteca to show that internal rhetoric happens unconsciously as well as consciously. In this chapter, Mead and Vygotsky provide the basis for claiming that our very selves are rhetorically constituted by arguing that language evolution and development necessarily involve the internalization of the hortatory function of language. Although this book's historical sampling of internal rhetoric is far from complete, it provides enough models of the various ways that internal rhetoric has been portrayed to move on to my conclusion, in which I explore how a theory of internal rhetoric and the rhetorical self furthers contemporary explanations of rhetoric and the self.

Conclusion: The Rhetorical Self and Moral Agency

> In each of us two powers preside, one male, one female; and in the man's brain, the man predominates over the woman, and in the woman's brain, the woman predominates over the man. The normal and comfortable state of being is that the two live in harmony together, spiritually cooperating. If one is a man, still the woman part of the brain must have effect; and a woman also must have intercourse with the man in her. Coleridge perhaps meant this when he said that a great mind is androgynous. It is when this fusion takes place that the mind is fully fertilised and uses all its faculties.
>
> —Virginia Woolf, *A Room of One's Own*

I must finally close this exploration of internal rhetoric, however provisionally. I have not completely "onionised" the concept of internal rhetoric. There are many more texts from diverse fields—the traditional rhetorical canon, philosophy, psychology, cultural studies, literature, pop culture—that can add to a more fully historicized and theorized concept of internal rhetoric. My goals for this book have been twofold: First, I wanted to open up internal rhetoric as a field of inquiry, providing enough reference points to indicate the potential richness of internal rhetoric as an analytical approach and encouraging further study of its historical and theoretical ramifications. Second, and perhaps more important, I wanted to expand and complicate the field of rhetoric, challenging the discipline to reexamine its connections to ethics and psychology.

I have argued that rhetoric provides a productive lens through which to view two phenomena widely recognized in our culture. First, social language practices shape identities or selves through internalization and transmutation into what I call *primary* internal rhetoric, a process that goes on virtually all the time in our subconscious minds. Second, I characterize the practice of talking to oneself as *cultivated* internal rhetoric, which rises to consciousness when circumstances warrant. Although it is useful to separate primary from cultivated internal rhetoric for analytic purposes, in practice the two are not so easily distinguished. An example from Mary Chesnut's private journal illustrates the complexity of internal rhetoric:

> I saw to day a sale of Negroes—Mulatto women in *silk dresses*—one girl was on the stand. Nice looking—like my Nancy—she looked as coy and pleased as the bidder. South Carolina slave holder as I am my very soul sickened—it is too dreadful. I tried to reason—this is not worse than the willing sale most women make of themselves in marriage—nor can the consequences be worse. The Bible authorizes marriage & slavery—poor women! poor slaves! (Woodward and Buhlenfeld 21)

At the most conscious level, Chesnut tries to use an argument from authority (the Bible) and an analogy to justify the sale of slave women for sexual purposes—and, evidently, fails, because she instead assimilates marriage to slavery rather than vice versa. What she is blind to, despite her claim that her "soul sickened," is that her analogy minimizes the radical differences between upper-class women and slave women in opportunities for choice about, and in consequences of, sexual activity. These assumptions, that all women are passive in their relations with men and at the same time responsible for their own actions, are two voices in the primary internal rhetoric generated precisely by Chesnut's position as a "South Carolina slave holder." The perspective given by internal rhetoric thus allows us to analyze private writing (as well as other sources) for its potential or actual effect on the rhetor herself, with sources of the rhetoric ranging from the apparent intentions of the author to the larger societal discourses of which she unconsciously partakes.

At a disciplinary level, the study of internal rhetoric bridges the gap between the traditional and expansive rhetorics I outline in the introduction. In between the traditional view of rhetoric as crafted, persuasive language in a public setting and the expansive view of "rhetoricality" as the way that language pervades and conditions our human existence is the perspective of internal rhetoric, which focuses on that moment when personal language takes up and reflects, modifies, or resists the various social languages that pervade our selves and our environments. It is unproductive to create a binary opposition between traditional rhetorics, which view the rhetor as the producer of intentionally crafted language, and expansive rhetorics, which see societal discourses or rhetoricality as determining our very beings. Rather, internal rhetoric points us toward a more nuanced understanding of how rhetorical intent *and* effect are discernible at every level of language use, and each human being is a site of both rhetorical dissension *and* concerted rhetorical action.

Neither is there a real dichotomy between internal and external rhetorics, because internal rhetoric involves interiorized social voices similar to those that shape external rhetoric. The social milieu operates as a constraint on external (public and private) rhetoric, but just as much so in internal rhetoric either through social mores invoked by Mead's "me" or by shaping cognitive processes into socially determined patterns. This does not mean that social norms determine the course of internal rhetoric, any more than they univocally determine external rhetoric. But social norms illuminate choices, create paths of least resistance, shape visions of reality terministically, and provide one of the important scenes in which a person acts and reacts.

The concept of internal rhetoric is of more than disciplinary relevance, because it also offers a rapprochement between rhetoric and psychology and between rhetoric and philosophy. Internal rhetoric invites rhetoricians to pay more attention to the psychology of both the reception and production of rhetoric, and it invites psychologists to recognize the extent to which the sociolinguistic shaping of the mind is rhetorical. To this conversation I offer the rhetorical self, the product-in-continuous-process of primary internal rhetoric. I then demonstrate how the traditional view of cultivated internal rhetoric as deliberate moral reasoning fits in the context of this contemporary rhetorical self, thus helping to mend the rift between rhetoric and philosophy that has existed since Plato questioned the ethics of rhetoric. In both cases, highlighting the rhetorical function of self-talk allows rhetoricians, psychologists, and philosophers to use pragmatic rhetorical concepts developed over many centuries to analyze identity construction and moral agency.

The Rhetorical Self

The rhetorical self is made up of a colloquy of internalized social languages, interacting rhetorically to adapt attitude and behavior to personal, cultural, and environmental demands. Although I draw largely on twentieth-century theorists for this assertion, it correlates with earlier portrayals of internal rhetoric, such as those in the *Iliad,* in which the heroes weigh various cultural and situational imperatives to figure out what to do. Hector, for example, imagines these imperatives in the persons of Trojan men and women reproaching him or as Achilleus shaming him pitilessly.

Although these personified, internalized social languages are complex, I will refer to them as "voices" as a shorthand for the many ways they are manifest. At the extreme of differentiation, they constitute interactive inner selves, which may be experienced and characterized imagistically and emotionally as well as linguistically. Voices can also be thought of as Mead's "generalized other," the various social contexts that create templates for acceptable behavior—or as the imperatives or social rules for action themselves. The rhetorical self and its voices are shaped by their immersion into language practices particular to both personal history and sociohistorical context, but they are not determined by them.

These language practices are internalized precisely because of their suasory power. From an early age, we learn that gestures (and eventually language) influence people around us; likewise, we are shaped by the hortatory gestures, language, and images that tell us how we are to be in the world. While not excluding the influence of other language functions (e.g., cognitive, narrative) that we internalize, I use the rhetorical self as a terministic screen to emphasize the primary nature of suasion in constructing and perpetuating our selves-in-society. As the social languages that constitute the rhetorical self are largely hortatory, so the internal negotiations among voices, within the rhetorical self, replicate and modify the societal rhetorics around them. Kenneth Burke's characterization of the "complex individual" having a "parliamentary wrangle" in her psyche (*Rhetoric* 38) is thus a telling metaphor for the operation of the rhetorical self.

The rhetorical self thus consciously and unconsciously practices rhetoric within itself, among its constituent voices, both to maintain a fragile equilibrium of personal identity and to resolve ambiguous or conflicting imperatives for attitude, decision, and action (which I will discuss in the following section on moral agency). Going beyond skeptical philosophers from David Hume to Paul Smith, who argue that our perceptions of having a continuous self are illusory, I account for this experience of personal continuity by claiming that a significant portion of primary internal rhetoric functions to maintain a tentative equilibrium among the voices of the rhetorical self.

People have a sense of personal "normality" when—and as long as—situations they inhabit allow a relatively stable pattern of rhetorical activity among their voices. Certain voices may dominate at particular times in our lives: in my case, for example, my familial ("dutiful daughter"), student, and working-class voices have all been dominant at various times. Some voices are so deeply and unconsciously ingrained in us that we are unaware of their effect on our internal rhetoric, just as Toril Moi argues that writers can never be fully aware of their own positionality:

> We cannot fully grasp our own 'horizon of understanding': there will always be unstated blindspots, fundamental presuppositions and 'pre-understandings' of which we are unaware. . . . The most powerful motivations of our psyche often turn out to be those we have most deeply repressed. (44)

Thus, while I know intellectually that I have a white privileged voice, I am unaware of its powerful rhetoric until and unless situations call its assumptions into question. The temporary equilibrium that allows me to "feel like myself" is thus a particular balance among voices at all levels of consciousness and unconsciousness.

Calling the state of feeling normal a "temporary equilibrium" does not mean that voices are all of equal rhetorical power in shaping the rhetorical self. Just as we respond to the claims of various public rhetorics with variable levels of adherence, we adhere to voices in varying degrees, depending on both personal history and immediate situation.[1] The primary internal rhetoric that shapes the rhetorical self is typically a conservative psychic mechanism, adhering most to the most deeply ingrained voices and often taking years (if ever) to internalize or adhere to new voices that are called forth when people enter new social situations or discourses.

At the same time, primary internal rhetoric is also the mechanism through which new voices are incorporated into the rhetorical self. When a new voice (e.g., English professor) comes along, it may cause an abrupt destabilization of primary internal rhetoric or insinuate itself into the already existing internally rhetorical situation. In either case, the norm of the rhetorical self changes or shifts: The rhetorical power of existing voices may strengthen or weaken, depending on how the new voice fits into the existing rhetorical self.[2] At times, there is such an extreme discontinuity of voices that one has a sense of becoming a "different person." Postmodernist terminologies focus on this discontinuity, which they characterize as radical fragmentation:

> The fully unified, completed, secure and coherent identity is a fantasy. Instead, as the systems of meaning and cultural representation multiply, we are confronted by a bewildering, fleeting multiplicity of possible identities, any one of which we could identify with—at least temporarily. (Hall 277)

In ignoring the ways that the self *is* continuous—through memory[3] or the normalizing tendency of the rhetorical self—postmodernism divorces itself from most people's subjective experiences.[4] The rhetorical self is less abstruse: what we experience as a continuous self is not, as Stuart Hall claims, a "comforting story or a 'narrative of the self'" (277) but a result of the ongoing primary internal rhetoric that negotiates "normality" among voices acquired at and persisting through various times in our lives.

The rhetorical self explains how we can experience our "selves" as both unified and contentious in that much psychic energy is expended on negotiating a comfort zone between the extremes of psychological unity (obsession, monologism) and diversity (schizophrenia, multiple personality disorder).[5] If people are socially constructed into multiple, often contradictory voices, then internal rhetoric allows us to maintain various degrees of coordination among those voices, giving us that sense of the continuous "I" that postmodernists consider fictive.

Thus, the rhetorical self (in the singular) denotes not a unitary self but a collective self: the repertoire of inner voices that people have to draw on at any particular time, in all situations, in their lives. What this rhetorical collective implies is a common ground, an agora of the psyche, in which these differing voices work out which attitudes and actions a person will take. And while internal rhetoric takes place within the larger scene of ongoing cultural and interpersonal discourses, its immediate scene is the biological organism, a physical substratum that conditions and sometimes takes over the rhetorical interaction among socially constructed voices.

Even in a humanistic study, it is important not to deny the effect of the body on internal rhetoric and the rhetorical self, as postmodernists like Stuart Hall tend to do: "The post-modern subject

. . . is historically, *not* biologically defined" (277; emphasis added). To avoid an overintellectualized view of the rhetorical self, I want at least to acknowledge that the physical and chemical environment of the brain influences internal rhetoric and thus the rhetorical self. Not only do naturally occurring chemical variations alter the mental landscape,[6] but humans (as well as other animals) also deliberately manipulate brain chemistry and moods by ingesting psychoactive substances.[7] From coffee beans to peyote, from laudanum to Prozac, people have adjusted their (our) mental states—changing the nature of their (our) internal rhetoric—for thousands of years. Brain chemistry may not be a rhetorical phenomenon, but anyone who has experienced depression, for example, will attest that brain chemistry plays a sometimes crucial role in the nature of the depressed person's internal rhetoric. More urgent biological forces may also affect our internal rhetoric, such as the body's reaction to immediate danger or, as Plato portrays, the animal passions' response to an object of desire. Our physical beings—with their assigned cultural values[8]—thus join other cultural rhetorics and personal history in shaping and reshaping rhetorical selves.

The rhetorical self is thus, to a large extent, unconsciously acquired and maintained: We are exposed to familial expectations and positionings long before we are self-conscious, and throughout life we are continually barraged by societal messages about whom we should be as teenagers, physical bodies, women or men, consumers, citizens, workers, and so forth. These pervasive messages are internalized and transmuted, creating primary internal rhetoric that does more than passively echo the cultural voices around us, but actively selects and adjusts these voices according to personal history and circumstance.

Internal Rhetoric and Moral Agency

In addition to the effects of culture, personal history, and biology on primary internal rhetoric, people have also cultivated specifically directed internal rhetoric that promotes certain values, interests, and behaviors over others. In other words, we become moral agents when we associate our inner voices and actions with a hierarchy of values and when we try to normalize our constituent internal rhetoric and behaviors to desired patterns. In this section, I address two questions: How does cultivated internal rhetoric explain moral agency in the framework of the rhetorical self? And, more importantly, how can cultivated internal rhetoric promote ethical behavior when there is little societal consensus on what is moral or ethical?

In part one of this book, cultivated internal rhetoric is associated with the psychic dominance of "Reason" in faculty psychology. Plato, Aristotle, Bacon, and Shaftesbury all argue that Reason is the only legitimate internal rhetor, with the emotions usually playing an adversarial role when it comes to making ethical decisions. Whately, writing after the Scottish moral sense philosophers and in the midst of British Romanticism, argues that "rational and *rightly directed*" emotions are crucial to moral reasoning (*Elements of Rhetoric* 180). These explanations depend on an agreed-upon hierarchy of innate faculties, something which current accounts of the mind do not have. Instead, social-constructionist views of the mind—including the rhetorical self—see it as built out of internalized social discourses or ideologies. Some accounts, such as Althusser's account of ideologies "interpellating" subjects,[9] are highly deterministic, even though they do not posit innate faculties. While the rhetorical self is not deterministic, the question remains whether such a portrayal of psychic parliamentarianism lends itself to explaining effective moral agency.

With regard to my second question, I hardly need to argue that we are in an age of moral pluralism. From disputes about laws protecting or denying "special privileges" for gays and lesbians to arguments about whether to teach creationism or evolution theory, evidence abounds that late-twentieth-century American society has fewer agreed-upon moral principles than do past or present societies with greater religious or cultural homogeneity. Alasdair MacIntyre sees this situation not as a recent phenomenon but as a product of our diverse cultural heritages:[10]

> In our society the acids of individualism have for four centuries eaten into our moral structures, for both good and ill. But not only this: we live with the inheritance of not only one, but of a number of well-integrated moralities. Aristotelianism, primitive Christian simplicity, the puritan ethic, the aristocratic ethic of consumption, and the traditions of democracy and socialism have all left their mark upon our moral vocabulary. Within each of these moralities there is a proposed end or ends, a set of rules, a list of virtues. But the ends, the rules, the virtues, differ. (266)

To posit the contemporary ethical problem as "how to achieve and enforce a universal set of moral principles" is unrealistic. A better question for the world we live in is "how can we, as a society and as individuals, make responsible ethical decisions in an era when moral principles are not agreed upon?" One answer to this and to the question about moral agency is cultivating internal rhetoric—not in the prescriptive sense of faculty psychology but in the sense of open-ended inner dialogue.

Isocrates points the way to discussing how internal rhetoric enables moral agency without recourse to absolutist definitions of the self or morality. As I argue in chapter 1, Isocrates claims that people who debate most skillfully in their own minds are the wisest. They develop the judgment necessary to grasp *kairos* and make the best decisions for meeting contingencies in their professional and personal lives. People develop *phronēsis*—a practical wisdom that guides ethical decisions—through a liberal education (Isocrates' *logon paideia*) that teaches them to exercise judgment and allows them to practice applying principles in context.

To extend Isocrates' claims for "those who most skillfully debate their problems in their own minds" (*Antidosis* §256), let me put them in the context of contemporary internal rhetoric. The rhetorical self encompasses numerous cultural paradigms for action and attitude, and people can be educated to allow these multiple perspectives to interact in the process of moral deliberation. Because it is often the case that cultural paradigms conflict or the consequences of a decision are not clear, weighing multiple perspectives is a way of making a "best guess." If people conduct their lives using a variety of ethical and cultural imperatives to steer through an infinite number of concrete situations, then open-ended (or open-minded) internal rhetoric—testing claims and predicting the broad consequences of actions from a variety of perspectives—is the only way to approach difficult decisions.

I am introducing a new factor when I claim that some internal rhetoric is "open-ended," but I am not advocating the kind of endless agonizing that Hamlet berates himself for:

> Thus conscience does make cowards of us all;
> And thus the native hue of resolution
> Is sicklied o'er with the pale cast of thought,
> And enterprises of great pitch and moment

> With this regard their currents turn awry
> And lose the name of action.
>
> (Shakespeare, *Hamlet* 3.1.83–88)

Rather, our internal rhetoric is open-ended when it is cultivated with the goal of allowing our many voices to interact in situations calling for decisions. One way to describe open-ended internal rhetoric is with Martin Buber's I-Thou relationship, "a relationship of openness, directness, mutuality, and presence" (Friedman xiv). Buber characterizes this relationship as occurring in "genuine dialogue—no matter whether spoken or silent—where each of the participants really has in mind the other or others in their present and particular being and turns to them with the intention of establishing a living mutual relationship between himself and them" (19), and he notes that dialogue can occur inwardly (4). Now, by this measure we can characterize internal rhetoric by the openness with which alternative voices are allowed into the conversation. In this ethic of relationship, the good is defined by what keeps our voices interacting and open to one another rather than by absolute principles that treat other voices as objects.[11] The value of cultivating this kind of internal rhetoric is that it makes us less likely to treat other people as objects, as instruments or "subject positions" defined by cultural success or failure stories. Carol Gilligan sees this morality of relationship as feminine (22); Perelman and Olbrechts-Tyteca cite Guido Calogero's argument that "the willingness to understand others, . . . the very principle of dialogue, [is] the absolute basis for a liberal ethic" (56). Open-ended internal rhetoric, then, is characterized by an open-minded willingness to persuade and be persuaded rather than a monological determination to force circumstances and people into predetermined moral categories.

It is precisely genuine internal rhetoric that differentiates kairotic decision making from pure opportunism, the kind of moral uprootedness that ethical absolutists tend to charge ethical relativists with having. Grasping the *kairos* of a situation does not mean only satisfying immediate interests, which a monologic, short-term thinker is likely to do. It means grasping the larger significance of the situation—its possible consequences and moral import. The mental habit that facilitates such considerations is internal rhetoric—polyphonic with the interplay among a person's ethics and socialization and the situation calling for a decision or action. I have already argued that the rhetorical self is composed of internalized cultural imperatives, which is one way that culturally approved values play an inevitable role in internal rhetoric. But we can also shape cultivated internal rhetoric so that the broadest possible range of interests and consequences are represented. Internal rhetoric thus has the potential to enable ethically constrained "opportunism" in a world where absolute principles are hard to come by.

But I do not want to leave internal rhetoric as the domain only of moral relativists, because people who are deeply religious and have strict moral codes by which they act still need to be able to apply principles to specific situations. Even in societies that are unified under a dominant religion, interpretations must be made to accommodate religious doctrine to specific circumstances or to reconcile seemingly contradictory precepts. Thus, the Catholic Church, during the medieval and Renaissance periods when it was at the height of its power in Europe, developed a flourishing casuistry or case ethics to decide on the application of church principles to different circumstances and activities.[12] Moreover, it is rare, in the United States at least, that a person who is deeply religious has not also been exposed to other cultural imperatives. For example, in 1999 there were a number of groups promoting the year 2000 as a Jubilee Year in which the outstanding debts of developing nations should be forgiven. We can expect to find bankers who are very serious about their faith but who balk at the idea that such a huge amount of debt should be written off at their shareholders' and customers' expense. This does not mean that they are unprincipled; it only means that there are numerous cultural imperatives laying claim to many areas of their and our lives.

The question of internal rhetoric and moral agency may seem a far cry from the proper consideration of rhetorical theory, but only if we accept Plato's divorce of ethics from rhetoric. Just as rhetoricians, in recent years, have argued that Plato's separation of epistemology from rhetoric is false, we must now explore the ethical dimensions of rhetoric by recognizing the concept and import of internal rhetoric. Instead of accepting Plato's limitation of our field, if we follow the Isocratean thread of refusing to split *logos* between speech and thought to Quintilian's definition of the orator being a "good person speaking well," then we are still in the proper realm of a more inclusive and culturally powerful rhetoric. In an era when "America's moral compass" is being questioned by conservatives and the very possibility of moral agency is being called into question by various postmodern conceptions of subjectivity, we must develop this rhetorically negotiated conception of the self and moral agency to take into account biological *and* cultural, conscious *and* unconscious influences on who we are, what we believe, and what we do.

Notes

Works Cited

Index

Notes

Preface

1. Some counterexamples to this generalization necessarily exist. The authors of *Women's Ways of Knowing* describe interviewing women who had been silenced by deprived or abuse-ridden lives:

> While we found in these interviews a few descriptions suggesting the barest experience of dialogues with others, there were no indications of dialogue with "the self." There were no words suggesting an awareness of mental acts, consciousness, or introspection. When asked to finish the sentence "My conscience bothers me if . . . ," Cindy, a pregnant fifteen-year-old, wrote, "someone picks on me." She did not comprehend words that suggest an interior voice that could give herself mental directions and exhortations." (Belenky, Clinchy, Goldberger, and Tarule 25)

Similarly, "wolf children" who grew up with no social contact and are linguistically deprived probably do not talk to themselves (Crystal 289).

2. I have chosen my epigraphs from popular as well as literary sources to illustrate the broad recognition of persuasive self-talk in Western societies. Although these epigraphs show the literary portrayal of internal rhetoric, which might be dismissed as merely an authorial device, the main focus of the book is how seriously the practice of internal rhetoric is taken by philosophers and rhetoricians alike.

3. Kenneth Burke also uses a functional rather than generic definition of rhetoric in *A Rhetoric of Motives:* "It is rooted in an essential function of language itself . . . the use of language as a symbolic means of inducing cooperation in beings that by nature respond to symbols" (43).

4. Scene in the Burkean sense: "when or where it [is] done" (*A Grammar of Motives* xv).

5. Gender intentional in the first two clauses. Anyone familiar with rhetoric in classical Greece will wince at the liberties I am taking with this encapsulation of its history: My purpose is not to provide an accurate three-sentence précis of classical Greek rhetoric, however, but to indicate a few reasons why rhetoric has come down to us as an interpersonal, mostly public art of persuasive speaking rather than as an art encompassing all of the original aspects of *logos*—speech, reasoning, and thought.

6. "Directing the attention" is Kenneth Burke's description of how terminolo-

gies affect people's perceptions of reality: "Any nomenclature necessarily directs the attention into some channels rather than others" ("Terministic Screens" 45).

7. Actually, Sayers also distances herself from the phrase, attributing it to "recent medical jargon" in *Busman's Honeymoon* (65)—but it's a great metaphor for what I'm doing.

Introduction

1. I realize that this use of the term *primary* may have misleading connotations, given George Kennedy's well-known use of the term to designate a very limited area of rhetoric: "Rhetoric [in classical Greece] was 'primarily' an art of persuasion; it was primarily used in civic life; it was primarily oral" (*Classical Rhetoric* 4). I use it instead to designate our pervasive use of language to regulate our psychological climates, a behavior that is prior to our development or learning of cultivated internal rhetoric. These terms should be more currently acceptable than the traditional philosophical contrast between nature and art or culture.

1. Classical Variations on Internal Rhetoric

1. This tactic is opposite that traditionally used by historians of philosophy, who dismiss Isocrates as a philosopher by using the Platonic criticism of rhetoric and definition of philosophy as frames of reference. See, e.g., Werner Jaeger on Isocrates: "To one who has just read Plato's *Protagoras* and *Gorgias* it seems obvious that the educational system of the sophists and rhetors was fundamentally an outworn ideal; and, if we compare it with the lofty claims advanced by philosophy—the claim that henceforth *all* education and *all* culture must be based on nothing but the knowledge of the highest values—it really was obsolete" (3:47).

2. George Kennedy distinguishes between "traditional or natural rhetoric," which is consciously rhetorical but not "conceptualized" or codified into rules, and "conceptual" rhetoric, in which techniques have been defined, catalogued, or conceptualized (*Classical Rhetoric* 6–7).

3. Modern historians of rhetoric are following a venerable tradition in citing Homer, as Brian Vickers notes: Aristotle, Cicero, and Quintilian all use Homeric examples in their rhetorical texts (*In Defence of Rhetoric* 3–4). As for the horses, E. R. Dodds points out Achilleus's horses talking to him against their *moira* ("portion" or "lot"; 6, 7) in the *Iliad* 19:405–19.

4. Jarratt cites James J. Murphy's first edition of *A Synoptic History of Classical Rhetoric* for the term *rhetorical consciousness.* In the second edition, Murphy and Richard Katula describe rhetorical consciousness as taught by Protagoras:

> Each individual receives the world differently through the senses, and then organizes those sensations into knowledge through an internal argument about the meaning of those sensations. . . . Knowledge is the result of this internal struggle, and . . . this knowledge is then challenged in public discourse as it confronts the knowledge others have attained through their own internal struggle with their own sense experiences. (31)

5. See Snell 6ff. for a discussion of the archaic Greek conception of mental powers. Snell's conception of Homeric psychology is reinforced and/or modified by several other authors, some of whom are summarized by Russo and Simon (483–86).

6. I have found eight instances in the *Iliad* involving five characters: Odysseus (11.403–11), Menelaos (17.90–106), Achilleus (1.188–93, 18.5–15, 20.343–53, 21.53–63), Agenor (21.552–70), and Hector (22.98–130). Whether these are all late interpolations, as Julian Jaynes claims (82), is not important to this argument, since I am trying to establish a tradition of thought rather than an exact chronology. Russo and Simon point out additional instances of "personified interchange . . . between a hero and his body" in the *Odyssey* (488–89), but I limit the present discussion to the *Iliad*, since this is the text most often used by historians of rhetoric.

7. Quotations from the *Iliad* are taken from the Richmond Lattimore translation. I consulted the Murray (Loeb) edition and Monro's extensive commentary to arrive at my transliterations and commentary on the Greek, although I do not specifically cite these sources in each instance. Definitions in brackets are from Liddell and Scott.

8. Monro notes that the aorist verb form "is used in impatient questions" (1:370). *Dialegō* can be translated as either "to consider" or "to converse with," emphasizing the dialogic perception of deliberation in Homer's time.

9. Lattimore obscures the formulaic expressions by varying them in each instance: the lines "while he was pondering these things in his heart and his spirit" (11.411) and "now as he weighed in mind and spirit these two courses" (1.193) are both renderings of *hēos ho tauth hōrmaine kata phrena kai kata thumon.*

10. Since the *phrēn* is mentioned only in this last formulaic phrase, the previous two having the speaker talking directly to his *thumos,* it is tempting to read the *phrēn* as the ego or self. I have not found substantiation for this point, however.

11. Fenik has a less generous reading, arguing that Menelaos's reasoning is an excuse that reveals his "important but secondary role" as a warrior (87–89).

12. Fenik acknowledges the difficulties inherent in claiming individuality for Homeric characters at the same time that he stands by his paradox of the formulaic coexisting with precise individualization (70–71).

13. Oddly enough, Achilleus also gives the same formulaic phrase found in the middle of the previous four speeches discussed—"Yet still, why does the heart within me debate on these things?" *('alla tiē moi tauta philos dielexato thumos')*—in a speech to the other Achaians over the body of Hector (22.385), while he does not use it in his soliloquies. It seems to signal a turning point in argumentation that does not occur in any of the Achillean soliloquies.

14. Obviously, the portrayal of internal rhetoric has different exigencies than those ascribed to the characters within the narrative. These demonstrations of internal rhetoric might serve a didactic purpose, showing the audience the "correct" decision—what a warrior with *aretē* would think and do—while allowing us to identify with the character's initial indecision. Russo and Simon have a different but not necessarily incompatible explanation of what they call the "personified interchanges" (488) of the *Iliad* and *Odyssey.* They argue that Homer's emphasis on the "interactional aspect of mental life" is "best understood as part of the poet's prefer-

ence for depicting mental activity in terms of common and public operations" (489). They are not arguing that there is no private mental life in Homer;

> Our point is rather that the private and internal aspects are not those that hold the greatest interest for the poet. . . . The various literary devices studied . . . all tend towards one common effect, which is to emphasize the communal nature of mental life and minimize the importance of boundaries or limits between the mind of one person and that of another. (490)

15. Russo and Simon caution that "we cannot be sure of the *exact* relationship between the vocabulary of mental life in Homer and all that Homer thought or believed about mental life" (486). They do argue, however, that the vocabulary reveals a "difference in emphasis" between Homeric and Platonic psychologies (486). My emphasis here is less to argue whether Homeric internal rhetoric is reflective or interactive than to demonstrate how early a depiction of a mental activity we can identify as internal rhetoric appears.

16. Jaeger disagrees with this interpretation of *aretē,* since he argues that "ordinary men have no areté; and whenever slavery lays hold of the son of a noble race, Zeus takes away half of his areté—he is no longer the same man as he was. Areté is the real attribute of the nobleman" (1:5). Jaeger's claim about the effect of enslavement on *aretē* is based on a passage in the *Odyssey:* "Slaves, when their masters lose their power, are no longer minded thereafter to do honest service: for Zeus, whose voice is borne afar, takes away half his worth *(aretē)* from a man, when the day of slavery comes upon him" (the swineherd Eumaeus to the disguised Odysseus, 17.320–23).

17. In the *Iliad,* there is a scene in which Andromache anticipates the death of her husband, Hector, from the noise of the crowd, just as Achilleus had the death of Patroclos at the beginning of book 18. She is not portrayed as talking to herself, however; she addresses her handmaidens and later the dead Hector (22.447–59, 477–514). Stephen P. Scully juxtaposes these two scenes in his discussion of the interanimation of speech and narrative (149–50).

18. I am purposefully resisting the modern urge to democratize here, although MacIntyre's assessment of *aretē* makes tempting the application of internal rhetoric for achieving *aretē* to all social classes.

19. Plato has Protagoras make a similar claim about his own teaching, which John Poulakos suggests is the inspiration for Isocrates' (113): "What I teach is sound deliberation, both in domestic matters—how best to manage one's household, and in public affairs—how to realize one's maximum potential for success in political debate and action" (*Protagoras* 318e–319a).

20. Yun Lee Too cites Jaeger as the source for this epithet (47n. 26); Takis Poulakos offers it as an accepted term (9).

21. The hymn to logos appears originally in *Nicocles* §§5–9, following a defense of *logos* in §§1–5. The hymn is repeated for the most part in Isocrates' late retrospective, the *Antidosis* (§§253–57). Since Isocrates is concerned about the criticisms of those who teach *logos* in the *Antidosis,* he makes more of a point that what is honorable to possess is honorable both to teach and to work toward. See *Antidosis* §§244–45, 250. He names Lysimachus as one of the critics he is responding to (§257).

22. My use of the term *rhetoric* for discussing linguistic activity in the *Iliad* was baldly anachronistic and thus clearly my own theoretical perspective.

23. According to Edward Schiappa, there is no evidence that the term *rhētorikē,* meaning the art of the *rhētor,* or politician who spoke publicly, was used before Plato's probable coining of it in the *Gorgias:*

> Prior to the fourth century *logos* and *legein* were used to describe what later would be called rhetoric. Both terms are far broader in their meanings than the term *rētorikē,* hence the appearance of *rētorikē* signals a new level of specificity and conceptual clarity concerning different verbal arts. (41)

Schiappa further argues that Plato coined the term *rhētorikē* to distinguish his own teachings *(philosophia)* from those of others, including the Sophists and Isocrates—and to devalue them (45). It appears, however, that the distinction was not commonly made, because the use of *rhētorikē* is still rare in the fourth century after Plato's introduction of it.

24. Through his uses of the present tense, in its habitual aspect, and the first-person plural and passive voices.

25. An observation that might be extended to his absorption in Panhellenism.

26. Although I do not want to add the anachronistic burden of the current Bakhtinian usage of *dialogic* to this analysis, it is hard to find another, less heavily connotative term for this to-and-fro, give-and-take *(dia)* sense of language use *(logos)—dialectic,* for instance, would entail the same problems, especially since it is a point of contention for studies of this time period. I will hesitantly use *dialogical,* therefore, to represent the nature of language as being a interaction among multiple users.

27. In the terms of speech-act theory, *euboulos* indicates the perlocutionary effect of the linguistic act of *autous arista . . . dialekhthōsin.*

28. Confirmation for this divided sense of self is found elsewhere in Isocrates' writings, where he, like Plato, uses the Socratic metaphor of the soul as a chariot: "When the mind is impaired by wine it is like chariots which have lost their drivers; for just as these plunge along in wild disorder when they miss the hands which should guide them, so the soul *(psychē)* stumbles again and again when the intellect *(dianoia)* is impaired" (*To Demonicus* §32).

29. *Noos* meaning literally "mind" rather than "wisdom."

30. See Michael Carter on the development of the term *kairos* and its roots in sophistic relativism. Carter argues that the meaning of *kairos* developed by combining *kairos* as the point of balance or harmony of Pythagorean opposites—maintained in the development of *dissoi logoi*—with Empedocles' and the sophists' concept of *kairos* being key to the arrival at probable truths.

31. This appeal to *kairos,* fictional or otherwise, has become a commonplace in academic prose, as writers and speakers refer to topics as being "outside the limits of this paper," meaning outside the *kairos* (inappropriate or untimely) for the rhetorical situation of the paper. This is particularly true in introductions, where writers must establish the timeliness and appropriateness of their argument to their audience.

32. Yun Lee Too argues that *Against the Sophists* is not incomplete but "announces

and enacts a teacher's attempt to avoid prescribing a singular, inflexible paradigm or discourse" (199).

33. In the *Phaedrus* 260a, the contrast is between truth *(alētheia)* and opinion (*doxa*); dialectic is associated with *epistēmē* at 266c.

34. *To Nicocles* and *Nicocles* are a pair of ethical treatises written for the Cyprian king Nicocles. The former, on the duties of a monarch, was probably presented to Nicocles shortly after he took power (374 B.C.E.); the latter, on the duties of a king's subjects, was probably presented somewhat later.

35. As many scholars have noted, Isocrates' "orations" were written with the fictional framework of a public address but were intended to be read as both pedagogical models and political argumentation. See, e.g., Jaeger 3:55, 302n. 27; Conley 17; Vickers, *In Defence* 10.

36. The simple story, that Plato is antirhetoric, is belied by millennia of conflicting interpretations of Plato. See my introduction to *Plato on Rhetoric and Language* for a description of the sources of ambiguity in Plato (2–5) and citations of other works treating related issues.

37. While the relationship between the historical Socrates and Plato's depicted Socrates remains an issue for both classics scholars and historians of classical rhetoric, most agree on the general principle that the earlier Socratic dialogues are more closely representative of the positions Socrates held than the later dialogues. See, e.g., Guthrie, 3:325ff. While not making any claims about whether opinions attributed to Socrates by Plato are "really" Socratic, I use character names to cite specific passages in Plato to avoid another pitfall in Platonic criticism: that of assuming that any character (usually Socrates) speaks transparently and doctrinally for Plato without regard to dramatic situation.

38. Indeed, James L. Golden argues that Plato puts "intrapersonal communication . . . within the sphere of rhetoric" (18). I am treading a bit more circumspectly around that point to take into account the derogatory things Plato says about rhetoric and knowledge (emphasized by Brian Vickers, "Plato's *Phaedrus*") as well as the positive indications that twentieth-century scholars can extrapolate from the dialogues.

39. On dialectic see *Letter VII* 344b, *Gorgias* 458a, *Phaedrus* 276e; on rhetoric see *Theaetetus* 201a–c, *Gorgias* 454e–455a, 464b–465a, *Phaedrus* 259e ff., 272d ff.

40. See, e.g., Black 369; John Poulakos 100; Vickers, "Plato's *Phaedrus*" 89–92.

41. See particularly Golden for a recent assessment of Plato's rhetorical practice. For the claim that the dialogues enact philosophical dialectic, see, e.g., Hyland 40; Swearingen 291; Poster 131–32.

42. Scholars have particularly noted the hypocrisy of Socrates' position in the *Gorgias*. See, e.g., Charles Kauffman and James L. Kastely for analyses of how Socrates breaks his own rules in that dialogue. Jyl Gentzler presents a different reading of what Socrates is doing in the *Gorgias,* arguing that he is demonstrating to Callicles (a) that he is an accomplished rhetor when he chooses to be, and (b) that sophistic eristics is a worthless enterprise.

43. Plato does have Socrates specifically mention persuading oneself, but in the context of eliminating a faulty way to think about knowledge:

> To put it in the most general terms—have you ever tried to persuade *[peithō]* yourself that 'Surely one thing is another'? Wouldn't the very opposite of

> this be the truth? Wouldn't the truth be that not even in your sleep have you ever gone so far as to say to yourself 'No doubt the odd is even', or anything of the kind? (190b)

Obviously, the question is rhetorical, and Theaetetus gives the only possible answer to Socrates' last question—"yes." Socrates is not arguing that we never persuade ourselves, though—only that we never try to persuade ourselves that one thing-we-know is really a different thing-we-know.

44. This is a somewhat misleading comparison, because *psychē* did not maintain the same meaning from Homeric times to the fourth century. For brief histories of the changing uses of *psychē,* see Guthrie 3:467–73; Popper and Eccles 159–71.

45. See Grube 130ff.; Dodds 213; T. M. Robinson 39–41. Robinson sidesteps the issue of whether the unitary soul is historically Socratic, concentrating instead on the development of Plato's psychology over the course of the dialogues (3).

46. Translator Paul Shorey notes that this view of the *thumos* is distinctively Platonic, different from the sense of *thumos* used earlier in the section on the *Iliad* (1:398 n.c.).

47. And indeed becomes so, in some Renaissance and Enlightenment accounts.

48. The three parts of the *psychē* from the *Republic*—the rational, the high-spirited, and the appetitive—appear to fit the chariot metaphor, but Robinson argues that the chariot metaphor actually represents a bipartite soul, there being no difference in the aims of the charioteer and the white horse (117). I would argue, though, that the white horse provides the motive force that puts the dictates of the charioteer into action—and thus the two divisions would be parallel.

49. Of course, "unhealthy" souls exhibit the internal dissension that might lead to an unethical version of internal rhetoric like the dark horse's. See *Sophist* 227d–228b; *Phaedrus* 237d–238c (although this is in Socrates' first, discredited speech); *Laws* 863b–864a.

50. See, e.g., Kennedy's 1991 translation of the *Rhetoric,* which he titles *On Rhetoric: A Theory of Civic Discourse.* Quotations from Aristotle's *Rhetoric* will be taken from the Kennedy edition. I have also consulted the Freese (Loeb) edition and the Roberts translation of Aristotle's *Rhetoric* at points in this discussion.

51. Aristotle uses two different words for deliberation, depending on whether he is discussing personal or interpersonal deliberation. In the *Ethics,* Aristotle is mainly discussing personal deliberation and uses forms of the word *bouleuō,* which has dialogical implications, as I pointed out in discussing Isocrates. In the *Rhetoric,* Aristotle is treating interpersonal deliberations, and uses *symbouleuō* and its derivatives—the prefix meaning "together, with" and thus emphasizing the interpersonal dialogicality. The distinction between personal and interpersonal deliberation for Aristotle is clear when he switches to *symboulē* to say that "when the matter is important, we take others into our deliberations" (*Nichomachean Ethics* 3.2.10).

52. Aristotle speculates much more about the operations of the *psychē* in *De Anima,* where he also divides it into faculties according to the various functions performed by living beings. He discusses how the *psychē* could be divided in different ways in *De Anima* 432a 23–432b 7. He sidesteps the question of what it means to say the soul is divisible in the *Nichomachean Ethics:* "Whether these two parts are really distinct in the sense that the parts of the body or of any other divisible whole are dis-

tinct, or whether though distinguishable in thought as two they are inseparable in reality, like the convex and concave sides of a curve, is a question of no importance for the matter in hand" (1.13.10).

2. Moral Philosophy and Internal Rhetoric from Bacon to Whately

1. For the discussion on Isocrates' view of rhetorical education, see chapter 1; see also Quintilian, 7:2, §29, 31; Blair, 1:9–10; and Campbell, lxxiv. I am arguing here not that Blair's overall rhetoric does not reflect faculty psychology but merely that his description of rhetorical education does not emphasize this influence.

2. I am using the term *philosophical* in its broad original sense of embracing natural science as well as the metaphysics and ethics we now call philosophical.

3. Bacon is using *tradition* in its Latinate sense, *traditio* as delivery into the hands of another; thus the purpose of the "Art of Elocution or Tradition" is "*to deliver over* that which is *retained*" (*Advancement* 261). All italics in quotations from Bacon are his.

4. This distribution does not mean that Bacon is a Ramist, however, intent on stripping rhetoric of any legitimate intellectual function. Bacon rejects Ramus's strict, exclusive classification of arts even as he proposes his own, similar classifications:

> And generally let this be a rule; that all divisions of knowledges be accepted and used rather for lines to mark or distinguish, than sections to divide or separate them; in order that solution of continuity in sciences may always be avoided. For the contrary thereof has made particular sciences to become barren, shallow, and erroneous; not being nourished and maintained and kept right by the common fountain and aliment. (*De Augmentis* 9:14)

The *OED* defines "solution of continuity" as "the separation from each other of normally continuous parts of the body by external or internal causes," citing another Bacon text where he uses the term in reference to the human body. Thus Bacon does not want his own classification of the sciences to be used as a strict demarcation of intellectual territories, as Ramus does.

5. This definition of "will" reflects Karl Wallace's discussion in *Francis Bacon on the Nature of Man,* 135ff.

6. Or rhetoric is used to mislead people: "It is wrong to warp the jury by leading them into anger or envy or pity: that is the same as if someone made a straightedge rule crooked before using it" (Aristotle, *Rhetoric* 1354a 24–29—even though he then gives detailed instructions for how to do just that in book 2, chapters 1–17).

7. René Dube argues that Bacon is intentionally revisiting Aristotle's systematization of rhetoric and response to Plato's critique of rhetoric (O'Rourke et al. 41–42).

8. For Bacon, this view of ethics or "Moral Philosophy" does not contradict the dictates of Christianity; rather, ethics acts as a "wise servant and humble handmaid" to "sacred Divinity" (*Advancement* 330).

9. Sir Philip Sidney claims that poetry performs this task of painting the virtues in striking pictures. See *An Apology for Poetry,* 27.

10. As Bacon writes with regard to Aristotle's "sophisms of rhetoric," "Their use is not more for probation than for affecting and moving" (*De Augmentis* 9:135; see also *Advancement* 301).

11. Bacon outlines this prospective science in book 7, chapter 3 of *De Augmentis Scientiarum* (see esp. 9:221–29), but does not go into the psychological detail he does in the section on rhetoric—at the same time that he blames Aristotle for "handl[ing] the affections" only "collaterally" in his *Rhetoric* and not in any of his writings on ethics (9:220). See also *Advancement* 329–46, esp. 338ff.

12. I use the English word *psyche* anachronistically here to avoid the narrower connotations of *mind* and the religious connotations of *soul; soul* would be inaccurate for the theist Shaftesbury.

13. Quotations are all taken from the Robertson edition of Shaftesbury's *Characteristics* and, unless otherwise noted, from *Soliloquy; or, Advice to an Author.* The latter is contained in volume 1 of the two-volume edition, so volume numbers will be omitted from citations to *Soliloquy.*

14. See, e.g., his criticism directed at epistemologists like his old tutor John Locke: "In reality, how specious a study, how solemn an amusement is raised from what we call philosophical speculations, the formation of ideas, their compositions, comparisons, agreement, and disagreement!" (1:194). Shaftesbury's concept of an innate moral sense is also contrary to Locke's *tabula rasa* doctrine. For a comparison of the two philosophers (and friends), see Brooks 434–38; Bernstein compares them with a different emphasis in "Shaftesbury's Optimism and Eighteenth-Century Social Thought" 90–91.

15. Bacon, of course, uses the term *affections* rather than *appetites,* but he is talking about that same "dark horse" which has been opposed to reason since Plato. Thomas Reid, writing a half-century later than Shaftesbury but within a similar ethical and psychological framework, explains:

> *Appetites, affections, passions,* are the names by which they [various principles of action] are denominated; and these names are not so accurately distinguished in common language, but that they are used somewhat promiscuously. This, however, is common to them all, that they draw a man toward a certain object, without any further view, by a kind of violence; a violence which indeed may be resisted if the man is master of himself, but cannot be resisted without struggle. (*Essays* 70)

This general, oppositional sense of an internally compulsive force not explicable by or amenable to reason or logic is characteristic of many, if not most, psychologies and ethics.

16. Much like Plato's portrayal of the urgings of the dark horse.

17. This is, of course, an ideal rather than a description of normal human nature. David Hume, in contrast, takes the extreme skeptical position that personal identity is only an illusion fostered by the association of chains of memories and perceptions. See the *Treatise of Human Nature* 259ff. Jerome Levin discusses Hume's illusory self in *Theories of the Self* 25–32.

18. For Shaftesbury, as for Plato and Aristotle, *natural* is a idealized term, reflecting a system in which "everything is governed, ordered, or regulated for the best, by a designing principle or mind, necessarily good and permanent" (*Concerning Virtue* in *Characteristics* 1:240), rather than an expression of statistically normal human behavior. Shaftesbury does, in explicit contradistinction to Hobbes, believe that people are naturally good. See Chapin 34; Brooks 432, 434.

19. Early in the treatise, Shaftesbury even warns his audience not to laugh at what he is about to propose (105), and he appears conscious during the entire work of the apparently risible nature of what he is discussing. See, e.g., 107–8, 207ff. This is the first indication, at least in the works I have treated so far, of the modern tendency to view "talking to oneself" as a comic indication of madness.

20. See Marsh 18ff. and Brooks 434 for further discussions of the opposition between innate virtue and corrupting society in Shaftesbury's writings.

21. Shaftesbury is, of course, here participating in the "Ancients and Moderns" quarrel popular in France and Britain, engaged in somewhat earlier by Jonathan Swift in "The Battle of the Books" (1704).

22. In this, Shaftesbury—like Isocrates and Plato—disagrees sharply with a school of philosophy critiqued by Alasdair MacIntyre: "All those recent philosophers who have wanted sharply to distinguish philosophical ethics as a second-order activity of comment from the first-order discourse which is part of the conduct of life, where moral utterances themselves are in place" (3).

23. In recognizing the rhetorical function of philosophy, Shaftesbury remains in the minority of philosophical writers during the eighteenth century, the majority of whom wrote in the "plain style" promoted by the Royal Society. Campbell, for example, makes this claim for his own writing: "Though his subject be Eloquence, yet, as the nature of his work is didactical, wherein the understanding only is addressed, the style in general admits no higher qualities than purity and perspicuity" (lxviii). Whately, too, although acknowledging that philosophical works are rhetorical in nature (5), denies his own use of rhetoric:

> As for any display of florid eloquence and oratorical ornament, my deficiency in which is likely to be remarked, it may be sufficient to observe, that if I had intended to *practise* any arts of this kind, I should have been the less likely to treat of them. To develop and explain the principles of any kind of trick, would be a most unwise procedure in any one who purposes to employ it; though perfectly consistent for one whose object is to put others on their guard against it. (xxxiv–xxxv)

These writers may be reacting against Shaftesbury's "florid eloquence," as Adam Smith does, while still acknowledging a restrained rhetorical intent for their own texts.

24. Christine Mason Sutherland introduces Astell to the history of rhetoric, arguing that Astell tries to replace the agonistic nature of traditional rhetoric with a more feminist, nurturing model.

25. The understanding and reason were usually differentiated in the seventeenth century, the former referring to "man's power of discerning and using the *forms* of

experience" (Wallace, *Francis Bacon on the Nature of Man* 96–97) or "abstracting and apprehending" (102) and the latter the discursive faculty of "analyz[ing], compar[ing], constrast[ing], and combin[ing] items of experience" (116). Astell does not seem to be making the same distinction; she discusses the understanding and reason together in her chapter "Concerning the Improvement of the Understanding" and calls the understanding "the Thinking Faculty" (89).

26. For Bacon's reconciliation of science and religion, see *Advancement* 6:91ff. Donald Greene mentions Shaftesbury's deism (93), which is described at greater length in Sambrook 31-32. Astell, too, is a high-church Anglican, but her proposal for creating a "Protestant Nunnery" was considered too "Popish" to be carried through (Sutherland 101).

27. Bacon explores ethics most thoroughly in book 7, chapter 1 of *De Augmentis Scientiarum;* Shaftesbury's stoicism is explored at length by Stanley Grean.

28. See the *Novum Organum,* aphorisms 1, 9ff., for Bacon's empiricism; Sambrook contrasts Shaftesbury's views with Locke's empiricism (53).

29. Bacon differentiates between "true" and rhetorical invention in *De Augmentis Scientiarum* 9:83–84.

30. See Locke 43–47. Locke is mentioned anachronistically in this survey of eighteenth-century philosophers because his theories play such an important role in that century. Greene notes that Locke's ideas "reigned virtually unchallenged" during the eighteenth century (100).

31. Chapin argues that Shaftesbury was more influential than Locke in ethical theory because Locke never wrote a systematic "Treatise of Morals" (33).

32. See Peters 436–43 for an account of the theory and significance of Hartley's psychology. Peters credits Hartley with introducing "the possibilities of a physiological psychology" (437) rather than the body-soul dualism dominant in European philosophy since Socrates. Hartley's psychology, in turn, enters rhetorical theory with the lectures of Joseph Priestley.

33. I am using the pronoun *they* to refer back to *women* reluctantly, since it reinforces the very objectification of women that Wollstonecraft is writing about; using *us* seems to project her criticisms (however accurately or inaccurately) onto the early twenty-first century, where they are wrenched out of the eighteenth-century context I am here drawing.

34. See *Vindication* 165, 200, 218, 238, 242, 257; *Mary* 51–53; *Wrongs of Woman* 86.

35. Shaftesbury, of course, is an exception to this as well as a few other rules. As I have discussed above, he sees internal rhetoric as "vanquishing" the insidious emotions by merely showing them for their true natures rather than aligning the emotions with the dictates of reason.

36. In his University of Glasgow lectures on practical ethics, Reid gives a sailing metaphor for the mind, reason being the helmsman that controls the course of the ship and the passions being the wind that moves it, in dangerous directions if uncontrolled (*Practical Ethics* 131).

37. Reid is not entirely able to eliminate the possibility of internal rhetoric, because he compares "the operation of the cool or rational principle" to the use of "*arguments to persuade*" a man to go from one place to another (74, emphasis added).

But clearly here Reid perceives this internal argumentation to be closer to logic, since it depends only on an appeal to reason and is opposed to the brute force of the passions.

38. While the need to address persuasion to both reason and emotions is a rhetorical commonplace dating back to Aristotle's time, the eighteenth-century rhetoricians update it with "scientific" explanations of the will and of moral philosophy based in the psychologies current to the time. Conley, however, cautions against assuming that the New Philosophy plays a major role in eighteenth-century rhetoric, arguing instead that "rhetoricians appropriated the vocabulary of the New Philosophy because they had already become convinced . . . that such things were precisely what persuasion consisted in" (190).

39. Quotations from Whately are from the *Elements of Rhetoric* unless otherwise noted; likewise, italics are his unless otherwise noted. He is here arguing specifically against followers of Locke in his claim that "the full importance, consequently, of Language . . . can never be duly appreciated by those who still cling to the theory of 'Ideas,' those imaginary objects of thought in the mind" (20).

40. See, e.g., Douglas Ehninger, "Editor's Introduction" xxvii; Einhorn 96; McKerrow 152.

41. See Campbell 77. Ehninger calls this the "'linear adjunct theory of persuasion'—the theory that in order to win belief or action the speaker must *both* convince the reason and move the passions" ("Campbell, Blair, and Whately Revisited" 175). Campbell and Whately are following moral sense philosophers like David Hume, who argues for a means-ends relationship between reason and the emotions (see, e.g., *An Enquiry Concerning the Principles of Morals,* 286).

42. Thus recalling the arguments made against the Stoics by Cicero, Bacon, and Shaftesbury and echoing Campbell's similar assertions (77).

43. See Smith 318–21, Stewart 6:20–31 on the distinction between reason and moral perception; see Smith 326–27, Stewart 6:28–29 on their doubts about whether people have a separate "moral sense."

44. This is the explanation Whately gives for whatever variation there may be among the moral precepts of different cultures or individuals—assuming, of course, that Protestant Christian ethics are the "uncorrupted" ones (*Lessons on Morals,* 3–4).

45. Whately's brackets. Campbell, too, considers the "moral powers of the mind" a sentiment rather than a matter of ratiocination (80), as does Hutcheson (Rendall 75). It is interesting that Shaftesbury also sees the moral sense as perceptual, but then posits an internal rhetoric based on the control of reason.

46. Of course, Whately is not the only person who acknowledges the inevitability or even positive nature of the passions, but he is the first source appearing in this history to see internal rhetoric as a discipline for fomenting emotions rather than just suppressing them.

47. Isocrates has been discussed in chapter 1. See also Quintilian, 7:2, §29, 31; Blair, 1:9–10, Campbell, lxxiv. Hutcheson gives detailed instructions on what countering examples we should imagine to alleviate each undesired emotion (165ff.).

48. Not surprising from an Anglican archbishop of whose rhetoric Ehninger writes, "First, and of overriding importance, it should be recognized that the *Elements* is predominantly an ecclesiastical rhetoric" (Editor's Introduction ix).

49. Isocrates believed that the two were synonymous, and it is his characterization of the orator that is carried forward in Cicero's and Quintilian's *vir bonum* ideal.

3. The Twentieth Century: Internal Rhetoric after Freud

1. A return to ethics in psychology is represented by Erich Neumann, who reconsiders the ethical implications of depth psychology in *Depth Psychology and a New Ethic.* He considers social phenomena such as wars and scapegoating results of the old rationalist or "ego-inflating" ethics and proposes a new ethics based on the integration of the whole personality. Neumann thus connects personal mental "health" to political and ethical relations in society.

2. See Peters 538, where Brett attributes to Kant "the real beginning of 'psychology without a soul,'" and 543, where he faults Kant for "separating ethics from psychology." Plato does compare, implicitly, the health of the soul with the health of the body in the *Gorgias,* but reverts at the end to a metaphysical explanation—the judgment of the soul after death—to explain why a healthy soul is better than a sick one.

3. Perelman and Olbrechts-Tyteca use the term *universal audience* to indicate the vain hope of a universally effective argumentation, not as a defensible concept. They argue that "everyone constitutes the universal audience from what he knows of his fellow men, in such a way as to transcend the few oppositions he is aware of" (33). Early readers of the *New Rhetoric* mistook their position on the universal audience; see articles by Allen Scult, John W. Ray, and Richard Long, and Perelman's answer to them in "The New Rhetoric and the Rhetoricians: Remembrances and Comments."

4. That is, Perelman and Olbrechts-Tyteca always qualify their assertions "from the standpoint of argumentation" (67), their syntax thus reflecting their philosophy: "We will stay clear of that exorbitant pretension which would enthrone certain elements of knowledge as definitively clear and solid data, and would hold these elements to be identical in all normally constituted minds, independently of social and historical contingencies, the foundation of necessary and eternal truths" (510).

5. Although Perelman and Olbrechts-Tyteca are writing specifically in the context of logical positivism, their argument serves as a corrective to many of the philosophers that have been discussed previously. Plato, Aristotle, Shaftesbury, and Thomas Reid, among others, distinguish between deliberation as a strictly logical or rational process and public rhetoric, which must include affective appeals to be effective.

6. Perelman and Olbrechts-Tyteca critique the philosophical privileging of dialectic at 35–40.

7. It is easy to forget that, before "rationalization" was usurped by psychoanalysts to show preference for unconscious motivations, "to rationalize" was largely a neutral or positive term for acts associated with the use of reason. The *Oxford English Dictionary* lists the following definitions (among others) for *rationalize*: to render conformable to reason; to explain on a rational basis; to clear away by reasoning; to endow with reason; and to employ reason or rationalism; to think rationally or in a rationalistic manner.

8. Perelman and Olbrechts-Tyteca define epideictic differently from Aristotle's original formulation of a speech about the present, the subject of which is praise or blame (*Rhetoric* 1358b): "The argument in epidictic *[sic]* discourse sets out to increase the intensity of adherence to certain values, which might not be contested when considered on their own but may nevertheless not prevail against other values that might come into conflict with them" (51).

9. Their conclusion strongly reiterates their opposition to philosophical absolutisms and reveals just how strongly argumentation informs their worldview: "Instead of basing our philosophy on definitive, unquestionable truths, our starting point is that men and groups of men adhere to opinions of all sorts with a variable intensity, which we can only know by putting it to the test" (511).

10. It is difficult to discuss or understand Burke's work without recognizing the importance Burke attributes to terminology. In the later essay "Terministic Screens" he asserts: "Even if any given terminology is a *reflection* of reality, by its very nature as a terminology it must be a *selection* of reality; and to this extent it must function also as a *deflection* of reality. . . . Any nomenclature necessarily directs the attention into some channels rather than others" (45). Thus, much of Burke's writing revolves around specific key terms (such as *identification*), working out the insights that each term gives us in interpreting our world.

11. Thus, in *A Rhetoric of Motives* Burke chooses the particular "terministic screen" of "identification" as part of a positive social agenda: "Because of our choice, we can treat 'war' as a '*special case of peace*'—not as a primary motive in itself, not as *essentially* real, but purely as a *derivative* condition, a *perversion*" (20). Like Shaftesbury, Burke is being consciously rhetorical in the exposition of his philosophy: "Books should be written for tolerance and contemplation" (xv). Unlike Shaftesbury, however, Burke emphasizes the connective rather than the agonistic functions of internal rhetoric.

12. See my discussions of Plato, *Phaedrus,* 254c–e (chapter 1); Shaftesbury, *Soliloquy,* 123–24 (chapter 2); and Whately, *Elements of Rhetoric,* 186–87 (chapter 2).

13. Descriptions of Freud's "psychical apparatus" may be found in *An Outline of Psycho-Analysis,* 145–47, and *The Ego and the Id,* 19–39, among other sources. It is interesting to note that in *The Ego and the Id,* Freud compares his parts of the personality to the faculties: "The ego represents what may be called reason and common sense, in contrast to the id, which contains the passions. All this falls into line with popular distinctions which we are all familiar with; at the same time, however, it is only to be regarded as holding good on the average or 'ideally'" (25).

14. Freud stresses the importance of dream theory to psychoanalysis in the opening of the *New Introductory Lectures:* "[The theory of dreams] occupies a special place in the history of psycho-analysis and marks a turning point; it was with it that analysis took the step from being a psychotherapeutic procedure to being a depth-psychology" (7).

15. Freud explains the purposiveness of the tendentious joke in two ways: "It is either *hostile* wit serving as an aggression, satire, or defense, or it is an *obscene* wit serving as a sexual exhibition" (*Wit* 693). "Tendentious joke" is the translation of James Strachey from the *Standard Edition* (*Jokes and Their Relation to the Unconscious*); I use it here as being clearer than *tendency-wit,* the term used in the Brill translation apparently referenced by Burke.

16. See Neumann 33ff., 137ff. on the suppression of the shadow. Compare this portrayal to that of philosophers like Plato and Shaftesbury, whose ethics depend precisely on the suppression of the "dark side" of the personality, that less amenable to conscious control. The difference in Burke's description is that he does not isolate the hostile intent in any one segment of the personality, but recognizes that in a factional situation such as the parliamentary model of the psyche (to be discussed below), any aspect of the personality can be the speaker with differing, possibly hostile intentions toward other aspects of the personality.

17. I am here using *scene* in Burke's dramatistic sense, incorporating his observations on scene and circumference from *A Grammar of Motives:* "The choice of circumference for the scene in terms of which a given act is to be located will have a corresponding effect upon the interpretation of the act itself" (77).

18. He also refers to the variety of motives an individual might have as a "parliamentary wrangle" (*A Rhetoric* 38).

19. See also Carl Jung's foreword to Neumann, in which he restates the same concept in terms of a parliament (17–18). Freud does use, without expanding on, the parliamentary analogy in *The Ego and the Id:* "In the matter of action the ego's position is like that of a constitutional monarch, without whose sanction no law can be passed but who hesitates long before imposing his veto on any measure put forward by Parliament" (55).

20. Compare this description with the unrealized complexity of Bacon's "negotiations within ourselves" and "confederacy between the Reason and Imagination against the Affections" discussed in chapter 2.

21. At the same time, his phrasing recalls Bacon's association of style with ethical motivation.

22. Also, Cynthia Sheard argues that Burke does not necessarily associate deception with immorality (300ff.).

4. The Construction of Selves by Internal Rhetoric

1. Donal E. Carlston engages in a similar task in "Turning Psychology on Itself: The Rhetoric of Psychology and the Psychology of Rhetoric," exploring the usefulness of studying the rhetoric of various disciplines.

2. My differences with Wiley and Hermans and Kempen are a matter of emphasis rather than disagreement. Both books use Mead to discuss thought and self-construction as internal conversation, as I do, but Wiley sees this as a semiotic, interpretive process, while Hermans and Kempen view the internal dialogue as a process of storytelling, narration—the dialogue, in their theory, is between narrator and narratee. Mark Turner also characterizes the mind as organized by stories, working from studies of image schemas in linguistics, cognitive psychology, and neuroscience. My calling the linguistically formed self a "rhetorical self" foregrounds the idea that the relations between the internal interlocutors function persuasively—but I do not rule out their semiotic and narrative functions. Yun Lee Too also mentions a rhetorical self with relation to Isocrates, but he means by it the rhetorical presentation of self (85–86).

3. Bruce Fink points out that Lacan's famous epigram, that "the unconscious is

structured like a language," refers to the contents of the unconscious as a chain of signifiers detached from their signifieds, their meanings (20–21). Because he uses Saussure as his linguistic basis (see *Écrits* 149ff.), Lacan is, like Wiley, more concerned with language's referentiality (or lack of it) than with the effect of language on human action, which is the core concern of this book.

4. Steven Pinker lists a number of features of human language—its grammar and specific areas of the cerebral cortex (334) and its "complex phonology, morphology, and syntax" (337)—that are qualitatively different from the many forms of animal communication that people think of as analogous to or precursors of language. He thus argues that, while language capacity did evolve, there are no extant species that exhibit early evolutionary stages of true language, and the evidence for specific linguistic abilities in extinct species are necessarily inconclusive. Pinker discusses the origins, evolution, and uniqueness of human language in chapter 11, "The Big Bang," of *The Language Instinct* (332–69).

5. For an overview of the 3,000-year search for the origins of language, see Crystal 288–91; he includes the "bow-wow" (that people imitated animal sounds) and "pooh-pooh" (that language was originally purely expressions of emotion) theories of language origin among the five named by Danish linguist Otto Jespersen (289). Rhetoricians have not been immune to the temptation of speculating about how language evolved: Adam Smith devotes Lecture 3 to the origin and history of language, and Hugh Blair devotes his sixth lecture to the topic.

6. Note that Kennedy's statement of rhetorical purpose—"aimed at affecting the situation"—is very close to Kenneth Burke's formulation of rhetoric aiming to "induce cooperation in beings that by nature respond to symbols" (*Rhetoric of Motives* 43), even though their discussions of the range of rhetoric are strikingly different.

7. In his book *The Expression of the Emotions in Man and Animals,* Darwin argues that expressions and emotions are not conventional but associative and biological in origin (see esp. 27–49).

8. Mead's discussion of instinctive gestures includes human behavior; he gives the example of feints in boxing or automatic moves of courtesy as gestures that are often not premeditated (15). An interesting turnabout is the "body language" vogue of the early 1970s, which popularized linguistic studies of nonverbal communication, making instinctive gestures significant through verbal interpretation. See Julius Fast, *Body Language.*

9. Mead modifies this stance later in his essay on "The Self" by arguing that language and significant gestures do not necessarily elicit the same response in the gesturing agent as in the recipient, but that they are *capable* of calling forth the same response, and thus the agent intends for these gestures (including language) to be received a certain way. See 147ff.

10. For the purposes of this argument, I will confine myself to human rhetoric, acknowledging at the same time that I agree with Kennedy's move to extend the rhetorical impulse to animals. My dog, Sheldon, for example, is a master of the pathetic appeal.

11. Plato also portrayed thought as internal conversation, but he saw this activity as *characterizing* the mind rather than *constituting* it. For Mead, the conversation creates the mind; for Plato, the mind creates the conversation.

12. That is, the development of the individual organism echoes the evolution-

ary development of a species. Linguists also compare language ontogenesis ("development in the child") with language phylogenesis ("development in the human race"); see Crystal 228.

13. I call composition theory a "related discipline" to rhetoric somewhat hesitantly, aware that the field of composition theory ranges from theoretical stances that are very dependent on rhetoric to stances that rely on a range of empirical methods.

14. Quotations from Vygotsky are taken from *Thought and Language* unless otherwise noted.

15. Vygotsky's association of the third stage with cognitive problem solving recalls the use of clarifying internal rhetoric in the *Iliad,* Isocrates, and Shaftesbury.

16. Vygotsky uses "verbal thought" as a broader category that includes "inner speech": "We can confidently regard [inner speech] as a *distinct plane of verbal thought*" (248, emphasis Vygotsky's)—contrasting it with "the next plane of verbal thought, the one still more inward than inner speech" (249). Verbal thought is what he calls the particular subset of thought that comprises the "higher" thought processes, while inner speech is derived from (but also distinct from) communicative speech. At some points he seems to use the two terms interchangeably: see, e.g., his use of the two terms at 88.

17. Actually, Freud's division of the self is closest to being sociohistorically determined, since the content of the superego is dependent on personal history. But the "fact" of the three parts of the psyche and the functions of the ego and id seem to be innate.

18. Assuming some kind of ongoing social contact. Stories abound of children growing up isolated from language, and in most cases their ability to pick up language at an unusually late age is limited (Crystal 289).

19. Vygotsky was a contemporary of (though not an associate of) Mikhail Bakhtin, who also discusses inner speech, but Bakhtin's treatments of it are primarily literary (see Morson and Emerson 163-64, 186, 192). Since I have already situated this discussion in Vygotsky's analysis of language development in children, I will base this discussion of inner speech on his presentation of it.

20. Vygotsky actually refers to inner speech as a monologue, comparing it to writing rather than dialogic oral speech (240). I think he is being a bit literal in that claim, ignoring the social embeddedness to which he attributes the development of inner speech. I am thus appropriating Vygotsky's views here to support my own arguments about the dialogical, rhetorical nature of internal speech.

21. Vygotsky is here referring to psychological rather than grammatical predication, a distinction he makes earlier in the chapter. Psychologically, the subject is always the known or given information and the predicate is always the new information, what happens to the subject, or "the carrier of topical emphasis" (221). In external speech acts, the grammatical and psychological subjects may not coincide:

> For example, in the sentence "The clock fell," emphasis and meaning may change in different situations. Suppose I notice that the clock has stopped and ask how this happened. The answer is, "The clock fell." Grammatical and psychological subject coincide: "The clock" is the first idea in my consciousness; "fell" is what is said about the clock. But if I hear a crash in the

> next room and inquire what happened, and get the same answer, subject and predicate are psychologically reversed. I knew something had fallen—that is what we are talking about. "The clock" completes the idea. The sentence could be changed to "What has fallen is the clock"; then the grammatical and psychological subjects would coincide. (220)

22. In contrast, written language is typically a low-context speech situation:

> It is addressed to an absent person who rarely has in mind the same subject as the writer. Therefore it must be fully deployed; syntactic differentiation is at a maximum; and expressions are used that would seem unnatural in conversation. (240)

Obviously, the distance between writer and reader are almost opposite the rhetorical situation of inner speech.

23. If Mead's technical use of common pronouns sounds unscientific, remember that the original Freudian terms for factions of the psyche— "das Es" (the it), "das Ich" (the I), and "das Über-Ich" (the over- or super-I)—are merely dressed up in Latin for their English translation. Mead may be adapting William James's uses of "I" (as "the sense of our own personal identity," *Principles* 1:318) and "me" (the "Empirical Self," *Principles* 1:279; see Hermans and Kempen 44–45), but he does not make the attribution in *Mind, Self, and Society.*

24. It is interesting to note that Mead's discussions of the game and social institutions (152–60) take place in the context of his discussion of the generalized other, which he does not seem to explicitly equate with the "me" but which he defines almost identically to the "me":

> It is in the form of the generalized other that the social process influences the behavior of individuals involved in it and carrying it on, i.e., that the community exercises control over the conduct of its individual members; for it is in this form that the social process or community enters as a determining factor into the individual's thinking. (155)

Wiley considers the "me" "committed to and merged with the generalized other" (47); Hermans and Kempen question that identification in their own reworking of the dialogical self (see esp. 115–16).

25. Mead considers his "me," the internalized social voices, to be related to but broader than Freud's concept of the "censor" or superego (255n. 8), but he considers the latter to be solely concerned with sexual conduct. In *An Outline of Psycho-Analysis,* however, Freud gives the superego a more comprehensive function: "This parental influence of course includes in its operation not only the personalities of the actual parents but also the family, racial and national traditions handed on through them, as well as the demands of the immediate social *milieu* which they represent" (146). This characterization sounds very much like Mead's "me." Wiley (47) compares the two, as do Hermans and Kempen (108). The significant difference between Mead and Freud is that Mead sees internalized social voices not as

constituting only one part of the psyche but as structuring the major part of consciousness and self-consciousness.

26. The amygdala is part of the limbic system, the most primitive part of the brain (Popper and Eccles 248). See Goleman 14ff. for a description of the functioning of the amygdala in emotions.

27. Just as Vygotsky argues that our higher mental functions replace animal "psychological processes" once we internalize social language uses (*Mind in Society* 57), Mead argues that the internalization of generalized others results in a qualitative leap in development: the child's "habits of response are reconstructed and he becomes a rational animal" (371). In the conclusion, I will use current studies of the biological aspects of behavior to argue for a biological self that participates along with all the social selves in internal rhetoric.

Conclusion: The Rhetorical Self and Moral Agency

1. "Adherence" is Perelman and Olbrechts-Tyteca's variation on what is known in traditional rhetoric as persuasion and in Burke's *Rhetoric of Motives* as identification, with an additional emphasis on its "variable intensity" (*The New Rhetoric* 4). I use it here to open up the spectrum of positions between complete rejection of and complete absorption in the voices we are offered or assume.

2. R. Radhakrishnan, for example, relates the complexity of his own "subject positions" as a citizen and academic displaced from India to the United States and from American and English literature (in India) to "theory and postcoloniality": "It is difficult to continue to historicize as though the diasporic move had not taken place, and it is equally disingenuous to behave as though the diaspora were a form of pure countermemory that breaks with the past altogether" (xiv–xv).

3. By memory, I am here referring to the synaptic changes in the brain rather than active memory. I discuss more fully the biological influences on the rhetorical self below.

4. The common experience of continuity is confirmed by the observation that we function—and expect other people to function—as more or less continuous sentient beings, responsible for most of our past actions as well as capable of planning future actions. The extent to which our selves are functionally continuous is indicated when we take into account extreme cases of discontinuity of the self, such as multiple personality disorders or Alzheimer's disease.

5. Much to the point, what I am naming "psychic energy" Kennedy calls "rhetorical energy" (*Comparative Rhetorics* 4).

6. For example, cortisol levels in the bloodstream vary with circadian rhythms and external stressors and are associated with "alertness, memorization, and learning" (Flinn and England 35). Regarding the culture versus biology debate, some scholars, like the physical anthropologist Lawrence Schell, are more interested in developing models of biocultural interaction than in zealously guarding more reductionist views of human life.

7. Peter Kramer, for example, tells the story of the development of chemical antidepressants in *Listening to Prozac* (47–66).

8. What our bodies react to as dangerous or desirous is not completely biologi-

cally determined but influenced by personal history and cultural attitudes. As Helen Fisher argues in her book about the biological bases of human mating behavior, "Culture sculpts innumerable and diverse traditions from our common human genetic material; then individuals respond to their environment and heredity in idiosyncratic ways that philosophers have long attributed to 'free will'" (*Anatomy of Love* 13).

9. As Paul Smith writes, "The problem, certainly, with Althusser's account is its stringent or, rather, uncompromising view, inherited from Marx, that the condition of dominated subjectivity is an adequate and full account of the 'real' subject/individual" (17).

10. In fact, MacIntyre is only unpacking the diversity within a narrowly Eurocentric range of heritages. The situation is even more compounded when we factor in African, Asian, Arabic, Native American, and other cultural mores.

11. Buber characterizes the "I-It" relationship as "the typical subject-object relationship in which one knows and uses other persons or things [or voices] without allowing them to exist for oneself in their uniqueness" (Friedman xiv).

12. Albert Jonsen and Stephen Toulmin summarize the history of casuistry in the Catholic Church in *The Abuse of Casuistry: A History of Moral Reasoning.*

Works Cited

Aristotle. *The "Art" of Rhetoric*. Trans. John Henry Freese. Loeb Classical Library. Cambridge: Harvard UP; London: Heinemann, 1967.

———. *De Anima*. Trans. W. S. Hess. Loeb Classical Library. Cambridge: Harvard UP; London: Heinemann, 1964.

———. *The Ethics of Aristotle*. Trans. J. A. K. Thomson. Rev. Hugh Tredennick. Intro. Jonathan Barnes. London: Penguin, 1976.

———. *Nichomachean Ethics*. Trans. H. Rackham. Loeb Classical Library. Cambridge: Harvard UP; London: Heinemann, 1962.

———. *On Rhetoric: A Theory of Civic Discourse*. Trans. George A. Kennedy. New York: Oxford UP, 1991.

———. *The Rhetoric and the Poetics of Aristotle*. Trans. W. Rhys Roberts. Intro. Edward P. J. Corbett. New York: Modern Library-Random House, 1984.

———. *Topica*. Trans. E. S. Forster. Loeb Classical Library. Cambridge: Harvard UP; London: Heinemann, 1966.

Astell, Mary. *A Serious Proposal to the Ladies for the Advancement of Their True and Greatest Interest*. New York: Source Book, 1970.

Bacon, Francis. *The Advancement of Learning*. *Works* vol. 6.

———. *De Augmentis Scientiarum*. Trans. James Spedding and Francis Headlam. *Works* vols. 8-9.

———. *Novum Organum*. Trans. James Spedding and Francis Headlam. *Works* vol. 8.

———. *The Works of Francis Bacon*. Ed. James Spedding, Robert Leslie Ellis, and Douglas Denon Heath. 15 vols. Boston: Taggard, 1863.

Belenky, Mary Field, Blythe McVicker Clinchy, Nancy Rule Goldberger, and Jill Mattuck Tarule. *Women's Ways of Knowing: The Development of Self, Voice, and Mind*. 1986. New York: Basic Books, 1997.

Bender, John, and David E. Wellbery. "Rhetoricality: On the Modernist Return of Rhetoric." *The Ends of Rhetoric: History, Theory, Practice*. Ed. John Bender and David E. Wellbery. Stanford: Stanford UP, 1990. 3-39.

Bernstein, John Andrew. "Shaftesbury's Optimism and Eighteenth-Century Social Thought." *Anticipations of the Enlightenment in England, France, and Germany*. Ed. Alan Charles Kors and Paul J. Korshin. Philadelphia: U of Pennsylvania P, 1987. 86-101.

Bitzer, Lloyd F., and Edwin Black, eds. *The Prospect of Rhetoric*. Englewood Cliffs, NJ: Prentice-Hall, 1971.

Black, Edwin. "Plato's View of Rhetoric." *Quarterly Journal of Speech* 44.4 (1958): 361-74.

Blair, Hugh. *Lectures on Rhetoric and Belles Lettres.* 2 vols. Ed. Harold F. Harding. 1783. Carbondale: Southern Illinois UP, 1965.

Britton, James, Tony Burgess, Nancy Martin, Alec McLeod, and Harold Rosen. *The Development of Writing Abilities, 11-18.* Ed. James Britton. 1975. Urbana, IL: NCTE, 1977.

Brooks, Garland P. "Shaftesbury and the Psychological School of Ethics." *Dalhousie Review* 62.3 (Autumn 1982): 431-40.

Buber, Martin. *Between Man and Man.* Trans. Ronald Gregor Smith. New York: Macmillan, 1972.

Burke, Kenneth. "Definition of Man." *Language as Symbolic Action.* 3-24.

———. *A Grammar of Motives.* 1945. Berkeley: U of California P, 1969.

———. *Language as Symbolic Action.* Berkeley: U of California P, 1966.

———. *Permanence and Change: An Anatomy of Purpose.* Berkeley: U of California P, 1984.

———. "Rhetoric and Poetics." *Language as Symbolic Action.* 295-307.

———. *A Rhetoric of Motives.* 1950. Berkeley: U of California P, 1969.

———. "Terministic Screens." *Language as Symbolic Action.* 44-62.

Campbell, George. *The Philosophy of Rhetoric.* Ed. Lloyd F. Bitzer. Carbondale: Southern Illinois UP, 1963.

Carlston, Donal E. "Turning Psychology on Itself: The Rhetoric of Psychology and the Psychology of Rhetoric." *The Rhetoric of the Human Sciences: Language and Argument in Scholarship and Public Affairs.* Ed. John S. Nelson, Allan Megill, and Donald N. McCloskey. Madison: U of Wisconsin P, 1987. 145-62.

Carter, Michael. "Stasis and Kairos: Principles of Social Construction in Classical Rhetoric." *Rhetoric Review* 7.1 (Fall 1988): 97-112.

Chapin, Chester. "Shaftesbury and the Classical View of Human Nature." *Cithara* 22.2 (May 1983): 32-47.

Cicero. *De Oratore. Cicero on Oratory and Orators.* Trans. J. S. Watson. Carbondale: Southern Illinois UP, 1970.

Cogan, Marc. "Rhetoric and Action in Francis Bacon." *Philosophy and Rhetoric* 14.4 (Fall 1981): 212-33.

Conley, Thomas M. *Rhetoric in the European Tradition.* New York: Longman, 1990.

Crystal, David. *The Cambridge Encyclopedia of Language.* Cambridge: Cambridge UP, 1987.

Darwin, Charles. *The Expression of the Emotions in Man and Animals.* Chicago: U of Chicago P, 1965.

Descartes, René. *Meditations on the First Philosophy.* Trans. Laurence J. Lafleur. 1641. Indianapolis: Library of Liberal Arts/Bobbs-Merrill, 1960.

Dodds, E. R. *The Greeks and the Irrational.* Berkeley: U of California P, 1951.

Eccles, John C. Part II of Popper and Eccles. 225-421.

Ehninger, Douglas. "Campbell, Blair, and Whately Revisited." *Southern Speech Journal* 28 (1962): 169-82.

———. Editor's Introduction. *Elements of Rhetoric.* By Richard Whately. Carbondale: Southern Illinois UP, 1963.

———. "On Systems of Rhetoric." *Philosophy and Rhetoric* 1 (1968): 131-44.

Einhorn, Lois. "Consistency in Richard Whately: The Scope of His Rhetoric." *Philosophy and Rhetoric* 14.2 (Spring 1981): 89-99.

Enos, Richard Leo. *Greek Rhetoric Before Aristotle.* Prospect Heights, IL: Waveland, 1993.

Fast, Julius. *Body Language.* New York: M. Evans, 1970.

Fenik, Bernard C. "Stylization and Variety: Four Monologues in the *Iliad.*" *Homer, Tradition, and Invention.* Ed. Bernard C. Fenik. Leiden: Brill, 1978. 68–90.

Fink, Bruce. *The Lacanian Subject: Between Language and Jouissance.* Princeton: Princeton UP, 1995.

Fisher, Helen E. *Anatomy of Love: The Natural History of Monogamy, Adultery, and Divorce.* New York: Norton, 1992.

Fleming, David. "Rhetoric as a Course of Study." *College English* 61.2 (Nov. 1998): 169–91.

Flinn, Mark V., and Barry G. England. "Social Economics of Childhood Glucocorticoid Stress Response and Health." *American Journal of Physical Anthropology* 102 (1997): 33–53.

Freud, Sigmund. *Beyond the Pleasure Principle.* Trans. James Strachey. New York: Norton, 1961.

———. *The Ego and the Id.* Freud, *Standard Edition* 19: 3–66.

———. *Jokes and Their Relation to the Unconscious.* Freud, *Standard Edition* vol. 8.

———. *New Introductory Lectures on Psycho-Analysis.* Freud, *Standard Edition* 22: 1–182.

———. *An Outline of Psycho-Analysis.* Freud, *Standard Edition* 23: 141–207.

———. *The Standard Edition of the Complete Psychological Works of Sigmund Freud.* Trans. under the general editorship of James Strachey in collaboration with Anna Freud. 23 vols. London: Hogarth, 1953–64.

———. *Wit and Its Relation to the Unconscious. The Basic Writings of Sigmund Freud.* Trans. A. A. Brill. New York: Modern Library-Random House, 1938.

Friedman, Maurice. Introduction. *Between Man and Man.* By Martin Buber. New York: Macmillan, 1972. xiii–xxi.

Gentzler, Jyl. "The Sophistic Cross-Examination of Callicles in the *Gorgias.*" *Ancient Philosophy* 15.1 (Spring 1995): 17–43.

Gilligan, Carol. *In a Different Voice: Psychological Theory and Women's Development.* 1982. Cambridge: Harvard UP, 1993.

Golden, James L. "Plato Revisited: A Theory of Discourse for All Seasons." *Essays on Classical Rhetoric and Modern Discourse.* Ed. Robert J. Connors, Lisa S. Ede, and Andrea A. Lunsford. Carbondale: Southern Illinois UP, 1984. 16–36.

Goleman, Daniel. *Emotional Intelligence.* New York: Bantam, 1995.

Grean, Stanley. *Shaftesbury's Philosophy of Religion and Ethics: A Study in Enthusiasm.* New York: Ohio UP, 1967.

Greene, Donald. *The Age of Exuberance: Backgrounds to Eighteenth-Century English Literature.* New York: Random House, 1970.

Grimaldi, William M. A. *Aristotle, Rhetoric I: A Commentary.* New York: Fordham UP, 1980.

Grube, G. M. A. *Plato's Thought.* London: Methuen, 1935.

Guthrie, W. K. C. *A History of Greek Philosophy.* 6 vols. Cambridge: Cambridge UP, 1962–81.

Hall, Stuart. "The Question of Cultural Identity." *Modernity and Its Futures.* Ed. Stuart

Hall, David Held, and Tony McGrew. Cambridge: Polity-Blackwell, 1992. 273–325.

Hartley, David. *Observations on Man, His Frame, His Duty, and His Expectations.* 2 vols. New York: Garland, 1971.

Hawthorne, Nathaniel. "Young Goodman Brown." *Nathaniel Hawthorne's Tales.* Ed. James McIntosh. New York: Norton, 1987.

Hemingway, Ernest. *For Whom the Bell Tolls.* Philadelphia: Blakiston-Scribner's, 1940.

Hermans, Hubert J. M., and Harry J. G. Kempen. *The Dialogical Self: Meaning as Motion.* San Diego: Academic, 1993

Hobbes, Thomas. *Leviathan.* Ed. Richard Tuck. Cambridge: Cambridge UP, 1991.

Homer. *The Iliad.* Trans. Richard Lattimore. Chicago: U of Chicago P, 1962.

———. *The Iliad.* Ed. D. B. Monro. 2 vols. Oxford: Clarendon, 1886–90.

———. *The Iliad.* Trans. A. T. Murray. 2 vols. Loeb Classical Library. London: Heinemann; New York: Putnam, 1924.

Hume, David. *An Enquiry Concerning the Principles of Morals. Enquiries Concerning Human Understanding and Concerning the Principles of Morals.* Intro. L. A. Selby-Bigge. 3rd ed. Rev. P. H. Nidditch. Oxford-Clarendon, 1975.

———. *A Treatise of Human Nature.* Ed. L. A. Selby-Bigge. 2nd ed. Rev. P. H. Nidditch. London: Oxford-Clarendon, 1978.

Hutcheson, Francis. *An Essay on the Nature and Conduct of the Passions and Affections.* Vol. 2 of *Collected Works of Francis Hutcheson.* Facsimile ed. Bernhard Fabian. Hildesheim: Georg Olms, 1971.

Hyland, Drew A. "Why Plato Wrote Dialogues." *Philosophy and Rhetoric* 1 (1968): 38–50.

Isocrates. *Against the Sophists.* Norlin 2: 160–77.

———. *Antidosis.* Norlin 2: 181–365.

———. *Isocrates.* Trans. George Norlin. 3 vols. Loeb Classical Library. London: Heinemann; New York: Putnam, 1928–29.

———. *Nicocles; or, The Cyprians.* Norlin 1: 74–113.

———. *Panathenaicus.* Norlin 2: 368–541.

———. *To Demonicus.* Norlin 1: 2–35.

———. *To Nicocles.* Norlin 1: 38–71.

Jaeger, Werner. *Paideia: The Ideals of Greek Culture.* Trans. Gilbert Highet. 3 vols. New York: Oxford UP, 1945.

James, William. *The Principles of Psychology.* 3 vols. Cambridge: Harvard UP, 1981.

Jarratt, Susan C. "The First Sophists and the Uses of History." *Rhetoric Review* 6 (Fall 1987): 67–77.

———. *Rereading the Sophists: Classical Rhetoric Refigured.* Carbondale: Southern Illinois UP, 1991.

———. "Toward a Sophistic Historiography." *Pre/Text* 8.1–2 (Spring-Summer 1987): 9–26.

Jaynes, Julian. *The Origin of Consciousness in the Breakdown of the Bicameral Mind.* Boston: Houghton Mifflin, 1976.

Jonsen, Albert R., and Stephen Toulmin. *The Abuse of Casuistry: A History of Moral Reasoning.* Berkeley: U of California P, 1988.

Jung, Carl G. Foreword. Trans. R. F. C. Hull. Neumann, 11–18.

Kastely, James L. "In Defense of Plato's *Gorgias*." *PMLA* 106.1 (Jan. 1991): 96-109.

Kauffman, Charles. "Enactment as Argument in the *Gorgias*." *Philosophy and Rhetoric* 12.2 (Spring 1979): 114-29.

Kennedy, George A. *The Art of Persuasion in Greece*. Princeton: Princeton UP, 1963.

———. *Classical Rhetoric and Its Christian and Secular Tradition from Ancient to Modern Times*. Chapel Hill: U of North Carolina P, 1980.

———. *Comparative Rhetoric: An Historical and Cross-Cultural Introduction*. New York: Oxford UP, 1998.

———. *A New History of Classical Rhetoric*. Princeton: Princeton UP, 1994.

Kramer, Peter D. *Listening to Prozac*. 2nd ed. New York: Penguin, 1997.

Lacan, Jacques. *Écrits: A Selection*. Trans. Alan Sheridan. New York: Norton, 1977.

Levin, Jerome David. *Theories of the Self*. Washington, DC: Hemisphere, 1992.

Locke, John. *An Essay Concerning Human Understanding*. Ed. Peter H. Nidditch. Oxford: Clarendon-Oxford UP, 1975.

Long, Richard. "The Role of Audience in Chaim Perelman's New Rhetoric." *Journal of Advanced Composition* 4 (1983): 107-17.

Lunsford, Andrea A., ed. *Reclaiming Rhetorica: Women in the Rhetorical Tradition*. Pittsburgh: U of Pittsburgh P, 1995.

MacIntyre, Alasdair. *A Short History of Ethics: A History of Moral Philosophy from the Homeric Age to the Twentieth Century*. New York: Collier-Macmillan, 1966.

Markley, Robert. "Style as Philosophical Structure: The Contexts of Shaftesbury's *Characteristicks*." *The Philosopher as Writer: The Eighteenth Century*. Ed. Robert Ginsberg. Selinsgrove, PA: Susquehanna UP, 1987.

Marsh, Robert. *Four Dialectical Theories of Poetry*. Chicago: U of Chicago P, 1965.

McKerrow, Ray E. "Richard Whately's Theory of Rhetoric." *Explorations in Rhetoric: Studies in Honor of Douglas Ehninger*. Ed. Ray E. McKerrow. Glenview, IL: Scott-Foresman, 1982. 137-56.

Mead, George Herbert. *Mind, Self, and Society from the Standpoint of a Social Behaviorist*. Ed. Charles W. Morris. Chicago: U of Chicago P, 1934.

Moffett, James. *Teaching the Universe of Discourse*. 1968. Portsmouth, NH: Boynton/Cook-Heinemann, 1983.

Moi, Toril. *Sexual/Textual Politics: Feminist Literary Theory*. London: Methuen, 1985.

Morson, Gary Saul, and Caryl Emerson. *Mikhail Bakhtin: Creation of a Prosaics*. Stanford: Stanford UP, 1990.

Murphy, James J., and Richard A. Katula. *A Synoptic History of Classical Rhetoric*. With Forbes I. Hill, Donovan J. Ochs, and Prentice A. Meador. 2nd ed. Davis, CA: Hermagoras, 1995.

Neumann, Erich. *Depth Psychology and a New Ethic*. Trans. Eugene Rolfe. New York: Putnam, 1969.

Nienkamp, Jean. *Plato on Rhetoric and Language*. Mahwah, NJ: Hermagoras-Lawrence Erlbaum, 1999.

O'Rourke, Sean Patrick, Don Paul Abbott, Marc Cogan, René Dube, Thomas O. Sloane, and James P. Zappen. "The Most Significant Passage on Rhetoric in the Works of Francis Bacon." *Rhetoric Society Quarterly* 26.3 (Summer 1996): 31-55.

Perelman, Chaim. "The New Rhetoric and the Rhetoricians: Remembrances and Comments." *Quarterly Journal of Speech* 70 (1984): 188-96.

Perelman, Chaim, and Lucie Olbrechts-Tyteca. *The New Rhetoric: A Treatise on Argumentation.* Trans. John Wilkinson and Purcell Weaver. 1958. Notre Dame, IN: U of Notre Dame P, 1969.

Peters, J. S., ed. *Brett's History of Psychology.* Cambridge: MIT P, 1962.

Pinker, Steven. *The Language Instinct.* 1994. New York: HarperCollins, 1995.

Plato. *Complete Works.* Ed. John M. Cooper. Indianapolis: Hackett, 1997.

———. *Gorgias.* Trans. Donald J. Zehl. Cooper 791–869.

———. *Ion.* Trans. Paul Woodruff. Cooper 937–49.

———. *Letter VII.* Trans. Glenn R. Morrow. Cooper 1646–1667.

———. *Phaedo.* Trans. G. M. A. Grube. Cooper 49–100.

———. *Phaedrus.* Trans. Alexander Nehemas and Paul Woodruff. Cooper 506–56.

———. *Protagoras.* Trans. Stanley Lombardo and Karen Bell. Cooper 746–90.

———. *Republic.* Trans. G. M. A. Grube, rev. C. D. C. Reeve. Cooper 971–1223.

———. *Republic.* Trans. Paul Shorey. 2 vols. Loeb Classical Library. Cambridge: Harvard UP; London: Heinemann, 1946.

———. *Sophist.* Trans. Nicholas P. White. Cooper 235–93.

———. *Theaetetus.* Trans. M. J. Levett, rev. Myles F. Burnyeat. Cooper 157–234.

Popper, Karl R., and John C. Eccles. *The Self and Its Brain: An Argument for Interactionism.* London: Routledge and Kegan Paul, 1983.

Poster, Carol. "Plato's Unwritten Doctrines: A Hermeneutic Problem in Rhetorical Historiography." *Pre/Text* 14.1–2 (1993): 127–38.

Poulakos, John. *Sophistical Rhetoric in Classical Greece.* Columbia: U of South Carolina P, 1995.

Poulakos, Takis. *Speaking for the Polis: Isocrates' Rhetorical Education.* Columbia: U of South Carolina P, 1997.

Priestley, Joseph. *A Course of Lectures on Oratory and Criticism.* Ed. Vincent M. Bevilacqua and Richard Murphy. Carbondale: Southern Illinois UP, 1965.

Quintilian. *Institutio Oratoria.* Trans. H. E. Butler. 4 vols. Loeb Classical Library. Cambridge: Harvard UP; London: Heinemann, 1969.

Radhakrishnan, R. *Diasporic Mediations: Between Home and Location.* Minneapolis: U of Minnesota P, 1996.

Ray, John W. "Perelman's Universal Audience." *Quarterly Journal of Speech* 64 (1978): 361–75.

Reid, Thomas. *Essays on the Active Powers of the Human Mind.* Intro. Baruch A. Brody. Cambridge: MIT P, 1969.

———. *Practical Ethics.* Ed. Knud Haakonssen. Princeton: Princeton UP, 1990.

Robinson, Daniel N. *An Intellectual History of Psychology.* Madison: U of Wisconsin P, 1986.

Robinson, T. M. *Plato's Psychology.* 2nd ed. Toronto: U of Toronto P, 1995.

Rogers, Martha "Patty." Diary, American Antiquarian Society, Worchester, MA. Also available in the microfilm collection, "American Women's Diaries: New England."

Russo, Joseph, and Bennett Simon. "Homeric Psychology and the Oral Epic Tradition." *Journal of the History of Ideas* 29 (1968): 483–98.

Sambrook, James. *The Eighteenth Century: The Intellectual and Cultural Context of English Literature, 1700–1789.* London: Longman, 1986.

Sayers, Dorothy. *Busman's Honeymoon.* 1937. New York: Perennial Library-Harper and Row, 1986.

Schell, Lawrence M. "Culture as Stressor: A Revised Model of Biocultural Interaction." *American Journal of Physical Anthropology* 102 (1997): 67-77.

Schiappa, Edward. *Protagoras and Logos: A Study in Greek Philosophy and Rhetoric.* Columbia: U of South Carolina P, 1991.

Scott, Robert L. "On *Not* Defining Rhetoric." *Philosophy and Rhetoric* 6.2 (Spring 1973): 81-96.

Scully, Stephen P. "Studies of Narrative and Speech in the *Iliad.*" *Arethusa* 19 (1986): 135-53.

Scult, Allen. "Perelman's Universal Audience: One Perspective." *Central States Speech Journal* 27 (1976): 176-80.

Shaftesbury, Anthony Ashley Cooper, third earl of. *Characteristics of Men, Manners, Opinions, Times, etc.* 2 vols. Ed. John M. Robertson. 1900. Gloucester, MA: Smith, 1963.

Shakespeare, William. *Hamlet. The Complete Works of Shakespeare.* Ed. Hardin Craig and David Bevington. Glenview, IL: Scott, Foresman, 1973. 899-943.

Sheard, Cynthia Miecznikowski. "*Kairos* and Kenneth Burke's Psychology of Political and Social Communication." *College English* 55.3 (March 1993): 291-310.

Sidney, Sir Philip. *An Apology for Poetry.* Ed. Forrest G. Robinson. New York: Macmillan-Library of the Liberal Arts, 1985.

Smith, Adam. *Lectures on Rhetoric and Belles Lettres.* Ed. J. C. Bryce. Oxford: Clarendon-Oxford UP, 1983.

———. *Theory of Moral Sentiments.* Ed. D. D. Raphael and A. L. Macfie. Oxford: Clarendon-Oxford UP, 1976.

Smith, Paul. *Discerning the Subject.* Minneapolis: U of Minnesota P, 1988.

Snell, Bruno. *The Discovery of the Mind: The Greek Origins of European Thought.* Trans. T. G. Rosenmeyer. 1953. New York: Harper and Row, 1960.

Sophocles. *Oedipus the King.* Trans. David Grene. *The Complete Greek Tragedies; Sophocles I.* Chicago: U of Chicago P, 1954.

Sutherland, Christine Mason. "Mary Astell: Reclaiming Rhetorica in the Seventeenth Century." Lunsford 93-115.

Swearingen, C. Jan. "The Rhetor as Eiron: Plato's Defense of Dialogue." *Pre/Text* 3.4 (1982): 289-336.

Swift, Jonathan. "The Battle of the Books." *The Prose Works of Jonathan Swift.* 14 vols. Ed. Herbert Davis. Oxford: B. Blackwell, 1939-68. 1: 137-65.

Too, Yun Lee. *The Rhetoric of Identity in Isocrates: Text, Power, Pedagogy.* Cambridge: Cambridge UP, 1995.

Turner, Mark. *The Literary Mind: The Origins of Thought and Language.* New York: Oxford UP, 1996.

Vickers, Brian. *In Defence of Rhetoric.* Oxford: Clarendon-Oxford UP, 1988.

———. "Plato's *Phaedrus* and the Reform of Rhetoric." Unpublished paper. Zurich, 1995.

Vygotsky, Lev Semyonovitch. *Mind in Society: The Development of Higher Psychological Processes.* Ed. Michael Cole, Vera John-Steiner, Sylvia Scribner, and Ellen Souberman. Cambridge: Harvard UP, 1978.

———. *Thought and Language*. Trans. rev. and ed. Alex Kozulin. Cambridge: MIT P, 1986.

Wallace, Karl R. *Francis Bacon on the Nature of Man*. Urbana: U of Illinois P, 1967.

Whately, Richard. *Elements of Rhetoric*. Ed. Douglas Ehninger. 1828. Carbondale: Southern Illinois UP, 1963.

———. *Introductory Lessons on Mind*. Boston: James Munroe, 1959.

———. *Introductory Lessons on Morals and Christian Evidences*. Cambridge: John Bartlett, 1857.

White, Bailey. "Dr. Fielding." *Sleeping in the Starlite Motel and Other Adventures on the Way Back Home*. Reading, MA: Addison-Wesley, 1995. 181–85.

Wiley, Norbert. *The Semiotic Self*. Chicago: U of Chicago P, 1994.

Wollstonecraft, Mary. *Mary, a Fiction. The Works of Mary Wollstonecraft*. Ed. Janet Todd and Marilyn Butler. 7 vols. New York: New York UP, 1989. 1: 1–73.

———. *A Vindication of the Rights of Woman: With Strictures on Political and Moral Subjects*. Ed. Ulrich H. Hardt. Troy, NY: Whitston, 1982.

———. *The Wrongs of Woman; or, Maria. The Works of Mary Wollstonecraft*. Ed. Janet Todd and Marilyn Butler. 7 vols. New York: New York UP, 1989. 1: 75–184.

Woodward, C. Vann, and Elisabeth Buhlenfeld, eds. *The Private Mary Chesnut: The Unpublished Civil War Diaries*. New York: Oxford UP, 1984.

Woolf, Virginia. *A Room of One's Own*. New York: Harbinger-Harcourt, 1929.

Index

Jean Nienkamp has published editions of *Plato on Rhetoric and Language* and Tabitha Gilman Tenney's *Female Quixotism* (with Andrea V. Collins).